Contents

Acknowledgements

I would like to acknowledge the invaluable assistance that I received from the following people in producing this book:

☐ Eric Addinall, for general advice and constructive criticism and, in particular, for writing the various computer programs given in Chapter 8;
☐ Stuart Allan, for technical advice, particularly on matters relating to audio recording and cine and video production;
☐ Bill Black, for technical advice on photography and for providing all the photographs used in the book;
☐ Margaret Geddes, for typing the manuscript;
☐ Anne Howe, for advice at the planning stage;
☐ Stan Keir, for producing all the illustrations;
☐ Barry Murton, for advice on computer-related matters.

I would also like to thank the many other people, both within and outwith Robert Gordon's Institute of Technology, who provided information and advice on specific topics.

Henry I Ellington
Educational Technology Unit
Robert Gordon's Institute of Technology
Aberdeen

The author and publisher also gratefully acknowledge the co-operation of the following organizations regarding the publication of copyright material:

☐ The Association for Science Education and Institution of Electrical Engineers (Figures 2.2 and 2.4);
☐ Control Data Ltd (Figures 8.5, 8.6 and 8.7);
☐ The Council for Educational Technology National Development Programme in Computer Assisted Learning (Figure 8.4)

☐ Phillips Petroleum (Figure 8.3);
☐ Robert Gordon's Institute of Technology and Grampian Region Education Authority (Figure 2.5);
☐ The Royal Bank of Scotland (Figure 2.6);
☐ The Scottish Council for Educational Technology and United Kingdom Atomic Energy Authority (Figure 2.7);
☐ SEDCO and Omnitechnology Ltd (Figure 6.2).

Introduction

In *A Handbook of Educational Technology* (Kogan Page/Nichols, 1984), my former colleague Fred Percival and I discussed the type of objectives-based 'systems approach' that should form the basis of all course or curriculum development work and examined the various instructional strategies that can be used to overtake different types of learning objectives. This book follows on from where the earlier book left off, offering practical guidance to teachers and trainers on how they can produce instructional materials to support their chosen strategies — covering everything from simple duplicated handouts and worksheets to the latest audiovisual and computer-mediated materials.

The present book is primarily written as a handbook for practising teachers and lecturers working in all sectors of education from primary to tertiary and for instructors and trainers of all types. All these groups should find it of considerable help in producing the supportive materials that they need in their everyday work. It should also prove invaluable to trainee teachers and, because of its comprehensive coverage of the field, should constitute a suitable basic text for students of education and educational technology.

Since the book is not based on any particular educational or training system, and deals with the various topics covered in fairly general terms, I hope that it will prove just as helpful to American, Australian and other English-speaking readers as it does to those in Britain.

The main text of the book is divided into eight chapters. Chapter 1 sets the scene for what is to follow by outlining the main types of teaching/learning situation in which instructional materials can be used, reviewing the different kinds of material that are available and providing general guidance on how to select suitable materials for specific purposes and when to produce your own materials.

The remaining seven chapters each deal with one specific class of instructional materials, offering detailed guidance on *when to use* the materials, *how to design* the materials and *how to produce* the actual materials.

Chapter 2 deals with printed and duplicated materials such as handout notes, worksheets and resource sheets, discussing the various instructional situations in which such materials can prove useful and giving basic guidance on matters such as composition and layout. It then examines the different methods that can be used to produce multiple copies of such materials and offers advice on how to decide which method to use in a particular situation.

Chapter 3 covers the general field of non-projected display materials, dealing in turn with chalkboard and markerboard displays, 'adhesive' systems such as felt boards, hook-and-loop boards and magnetic boards, charts and posters of all types, and three-dimensional displays such as mobiles, models, dioramas and collections of realia.

Chapter 4 deals with the various types of still projected display materials, looking first at overhead projector transparencies and similar materials, then at photographic slides and slide sequences (including the relevant aspects of photography).

Chapter 5 discusses simple audio materials, providing a basic intro- duction to sound recording, editing, etc and then showing how to design and produce audio materials for specific purposes — audiotapes for class or individual use, materials for language laboratories, etc.

Chapter 6 examines the various ways in which audio materials can be linked with still visual materials, dealing first with systems that link tape with textual and photographic materials, then with less well- known systems such as tape-model and tape-realia.

Chapter 7 deals with the two main systems that link audio and moving visual materials: cine film and video. In each case, it provides information on the basic techniques involved and guidance on the planning and production of the materials.

Finally, Chapter 8 looks at computer-mediated materials, dealing first with the various types of 'conventional' computer-based learning materials and then with interactive video materials.

In order to enable readers to study in greater depth any topic or topics in which they are particularly interested, a short bibliography is provided at the end of each chapter. These bibliographies list books, articles and other relevant materials that readers should find useful.

This book also contains a detailed keyword index to the material covered in the main text, which should help readers to track down any topic in which they are especially interested.

Finally, let me apologize in advance for the fact that I have made exclusive use of male pronouns throughout the book. This is not done for male chauvinist reasons, but merely to avoid breaking up the flow of the text by constant use of the rather clumsy 'he or she' and 'his or her'. Thus, wherever words 'he' or 'his' occur, they should be taken as covering both the masculine and feminine genders.

Chapter 1

A Guide to the Selection
of Instructional Materials

Introduction

In *A Handbook of Educational Technology*, Fred Percival and I argued that the first step in any systematic approach to course or curriculum design should be the establishment of clearly defined learning objectives. In other words, the teacher, instructor or trainer should try to specify exactly what it is that he wants the learners to achieve as a result of the instructional process. Once this has been done, the teacher, instructor or trainer should examine the various instructional methods that could be used to achieve these objectives and select the method (or group of methods) that he feels would be most suitable with the target population in question, taking account of all the relevant factors and circumstances. He should then decide what supportive materials will be needed to put the method(s) into practice and, if such materials are not already available, should set about producing them. The present book has been written in order to help teachers, instructors and trainers to acquire the knowledge and skills needed to carry out such a task.

When I started to plan the structure of this book, my original idea was to limit it to seven chapters, each of which would deal with the design and production of one particular group of teaching materials. On reflection, however, I decided that the usefulness of the book would be greatly increased if I added an opening chapter that would place the following chapters in their proper context by providing a broad overview of the way in which well-chosen instructional materials can enhance the effectiveness of the teaching/learning process. We will therefore begin by examining the different roles of instructional materials in different teaching/learning systems, reviewing the range of such materials that are available to the modern teacher or trainer, and offering guidance as to how to set about selecting materials for specific purposes and then acquiring or producing the same.

The Different Roles of Instructional Materials
in Different Teaching/Learning Systems

Since this is a practical book on producing teaching materials rather than a treatise on the theory of learning, I will resist the temptation to begin this section by discussing Skinner's stimulus/response model, Gilbert's mathetics, Gagné's categories of learning, the taxonomies of learning objectives proposed by Bloom, Krathwohl and Harrow, and so on. Readers who are unfamiliar with the basic ideas of these various workers, and who feel that it is necessary for them to acquire such familiarity before proceeding further, are referred to any basic text on the subject. The opening chapter of Romiszowski's *The Selection and Use of Instructional Media*, for example, provides an excellent introduction to the field (see Bibliography).

Rather, I will proceed directly to a discussion of the different types of teaching/learning systems as seen from the point of view of the practising teacher or trainer rather than the educational theorist, using a classification that I have found particularly useful in my own work. This classification, to which I was first introduced by Professor Lewis Elton of the University of Surrey in a seminal paper that he presented at the 1977 ETIC Conference (see Bibliography), was subsequently used by Fred Percival and myself in *A Handbook of Educational Technology*. It divides all teaching/learning systems into three broad groups, which may be loosely described as mass instruction techniques, individualized instruction techniques and group learning techniques (see Figure 1.1). Let us now examine these in more detail, and see what role instructional materials are capable of playing in each.

Class of techniques	Examples	Role of teacher/instructor/trainer
Mass instruction	Conventional lectures and expository lessons; television and radio broadcasts; cable television; films.	Traditional expository role; controller of instruction process.
Individualized instruction	Directed study; programmed learning; mediated self-instruction; computer-based learning (CBL).	Producer/manager of learning resources; tutor and guide.
Group learning	Tutorials; seminars; group exercises and projects; games and simulations; self-help groups.	Organizer and facilitator.

Figure 1.1 **The three basic classes of instructional methods**

Mass Instruction Techniques

This group encompasses all techniques that involve expository teaching of a class of students or trainees by a teacher or instructor, either directly (via a lecture or taught lesson of some sort) or indirectly (via an audiovisual medium such as film, closed-circuit TV, broadcast TV or radio). It places the teacher or instructor in his traditional role, namely, that of a source of information and controller of the teaching/learning process, with the learner being restricted to a more-or-less passive role and having to work at a rate that is entirely determined by the instructor.

Although there has undoubtedly been a move away from the former near total reliance on this mode of instruction over the last 20 or 30 years, it is still by far the most commonly used method in most educational and training establishments. The reasons for this are multitudinous. First, it is the method with which the great majority of teachers and trainers are most familiar and feel most comfortable, probably because they are 'in control' and do not have their authority challenged. Second, it is generally popular with students and trainees, probably because they, too, are familiar with the method and feel comfortable and 'secure' with it; most students, after all, are perfectly happy to be placed in a passive role that makes no great demands on them. Third, it can be extremely cost-effective (at least in purely logistical terms) enabling large numbers of students or trainees to be taught by a single teacher or instructor. Fourth, it makes timetabling relatively simple and straightforward — a feature that endears it to educational administrators who, in many cases, seem more concerned with the smooth running of their establishments than with the quality of the learning process that takes place therein. Thus, despite its many educational shortcomings (inability to accommodate different student learning styles and learning rates, unsuitability for achieving many higher cognitive and non-cognitive objectives, and so on) mass instruction will almost certainly continue to play a major role in formal education and training for many years to come. It is therefore up to the average 'coal-face' teacher or trainer to try to use the method as effectively as possible, something that can only be done (I would submit) if systematic use is made of appropriate supportive instructional materials.

Within the context of the various techniques that can be employed as vehicles for mass instruction, audiovisual and other instructional materials can play a number of roles. In some cases (eg the use of visual aids, handouts or worksheets in a lecture or taught lesson) their role will probably be mainly supportive; in others (eg film or video presentations or off-air broadcasts) they can constitute the essence of the method itself. In both cases, however, it is important that the materials be chosen because of their suitability for achieving the desired learning objectives, and not merely because they 'happen to be available' or because the teacher or instructor wants to 'fill in time'. Some of the ways in which instructional materials can be used in mass instruction are given below.

☐ Forming an integral part of the main exposition by providing 'signposts', guidance for note-taking, illustrative material, worksheets, etc.
☐ Providing supplementary material (background reading, remedial or extension material, enrichment material, and so on).
☐ Increasing student motivation by introducing visually attractive, interesting or simply 'different' material into an otherwise routine lesson.
☐ Illustrating applications, relations, integration of one topic with another, and so on.

As we will see later, a large number of different materials can be used to fulfil these various functions.

Individualized Instruction Techniques

Whereas conventional mass instructional teaching strategies are dominated by the teacher or instructor and by constraints imposed by the institution or system within which he operates, the various techniques and systems that fall into the class of 'individualized learning methods' are much more student-centred in their approach. These are designed to cope with the needs of individual students, who can differ greatly in such things as preferred learning style and natural pace of learning. A wide range of individualized learning techniques has been developed over the years, from text-based methods of the type used in traditional correspondence courses to the latest audiovisual and computer-mediated techniques. The educational and training contexts within which such techniques are used also vary greatly, ranging from the incorporation of specific elements of individualized or resource-based learning into conventional teacher/institution-centred systems to systems where practically all the conventional barriers to educational or training opportunities have been removed, so that a potential student can be of any age or background and can study in places, and at times, which suit the individual rather than the host institution.

Although individualized learning, in the form of correspondence courses and similar systems, also has a long tradition of use in education, it was only comparatively recently that it started to become an integral part of mainstream education and training. The catalyst for this development was Skinner's work on behavioural psychology and the stimulus-response model of learning during the 1950s. In many people's view, the latter constituted the first truly 'scientific' theory of learning, and triggered off the bandwagon programmed learning movement that so dominated progressive educational thinking during the 1960s. Indeed, while at Aberdeen College of Education in 1966, I remember being told by one programmed learning enthusiast on the staff that the traditional classroom teacher would soon become obsolete, being replaced by the wonderful new 'teaching machines' that were being developed as delivery systems for learning programmes. As it turned out, however, these teaching machines proved to be the biggest non-event in the history of education, partly because of their high cost and the failure of their manufacturers to produce high-quality associated courseware in the quantities that would have been needed to enable them to make any real impact, and partly because of the increasing realization that there was much more to education than the mere teaching of facts and principles (which was basically all that such machines could do). Nevertheless, the programmed learning movement has had a tremendous — and, I think, beneficial — influence on educational thinking, and has certainly led to a more widespread use of individualized learning techniques such as tape-slide programmes and computer-based learning, as well as to the development of fully integrated self-instruction systems such as the Keller Plan and Open University systems. Certainly, no progressive teacher or trainer can really afford to ignore individualized learning any more, since it constitutes one of the most powerful groups of techniques in the modern educational armoury — especially as a means of overtaking objectives in the lower-to-middle region of the cognitive domain and teaching certain basic psychomotor skills.

As shown in Figure 1, the role of the teacher, instructor or trainer in an individualized learning system is completely different from his traditional role as a presenter of information and controller of the instructional process. Rather, his role is that of a producer/manager of learning resources and a tutor and guide to the learner. Needless to say, some teachers and trainers — especially the older or more conservative ones — find it very difficult or even impossible to reconcile themselves to such a role. Also the role of the actual instructional materials in an individualized instruction system is radically different from that in a mass-instruction system. In the latter their role is generally supportive, with the main vehicle of instruction being the teacher or trainer in control of the class; in an individualized instruction system, on the other hand, the materials themselves constitute the vehicle whereby instruction takes place. Thus it is particularly important that such materials should be designed and produced with the greatest care for, if they are not, the system could at best fail to achieve all its instructional objectives and at worst break down completely. Much of the remainder of this book will be devoted to helping readers to make sure that this does not happen with any self-instructional materials that they produce.

Group Learning Techniques

While mass instruction and individualized instruction can be used to overtake a wide range of educational and training objectives, there are, in fact, a number of definite limitations to both approaches. For example, neither is suitable for achieving the full range of higher cognitives that are coming to be regarded as so important in today's education, and neither can be used to develop the various communication and interpersonal skills that a person needs in order to function effectively as part of a group. This has led to an increasing realization in recent years that the various activities that come under the general heading of group learning have a very important role to play in modern education and training.

The theoretical basis of much of the current interest in group learning is the humanistic psychology that was developed by people such as Carl Rogers during the 1960s — a totally different type of psychology from the highly mechanistic behavioural psychology which formed the basis of the programmed learning movement. Humanistic psychology is concerned with how people interact with and learn from one another in small-group situations, and involves the use of the techniques of group dynamics. When used in an instructional situation such techniques generally require no specialized hardware and, in many cases, very little in the way of courseware other than textual materials (booklets, briefing sheets, worksheets, etc); indeed, the emphasis is usually on the approach or technique rather than a reliance on specific types of hardware or courseware. Nevertheless, it is vitally important that any courseware that is required for such an exercise should be very carefully designed, since it can play a key role in making sure that the exercise runs smoothly — as I know from my own work on educational games and simulations. Some of the ways in which such courseware can be used in group learning activities are given below.

☐ Forming an integral part of the group-learning process by providing background information, information about roles, instructions, and so on.
☐ Providing supplementary or enrichment material.
☐ Increasing student motivation through visually attractive or intrinsically interesting material.

As in the case of mass instruction, a large number of different types of materials can be used to fulfil these various functions.

The Different Types of Instructional Material that are Available Today

Compared with his counterparts of 30 or 40 years ago, the modern teacher or trainer has a vast and often bewildering range of instructional materials at his disposal. When I was at school during the late 1940s and 1950s, practically the only teaching aids that were in regular use (apart from textbooks and specialized laboratory and workshop equipment) were chalkboards, wallcharts, posters and realia like geological and biological specimens, backed up by the (very) occasional use of slides, filmstrips, films, gramophone records and radio broadcasts, and (in the case of one art teacher) a somewhat antique opaque projector. I do not remember duplicated materials like worksheets and handout notes being used to any great extent; tape recorders were extremely rare; there were no overhead projectors or television sets (at least, not in my schools); resource-based and mediated learning had still to be invented; and there were, of course, no video recorders, electronic calculators or computers. Indeed, it is only during the last ten years or so that the overhead projector (surely now the most basic and essential of all teaching aids) has become a standard fitting in teaching rooms in my own college (Robert Gordon's Institute of Technology).

In order to help readers to become familiar with the main characteristics of the various types of instructional materials that are currently available – and give this book a workable structure – I have divided them into seven broad groups, in order of increasing technical sophistication. These groups are:

1. printed and duplicated materials;
2. non-projected display materials;
3. still projected display materials;
4. audio materials;
5. linked audio and still visual materials;
6. cine and video materials;
7. computer-mediated materials.

Let us now take a broad look at these various groups and identify the general characteristics of the materials that compose them.

Printed and Duplicated Materials

These comprise all textual and other materials that can be run off in large numbers on a duplicator or printing machine to be used by pupils, students or trainees. Facilities for the production of such materials are now available in practically every school, college and training establishment, and they have become one of the most basic and widely used of all educational tools. Some of the more important types are listed below.

Handouts: these comprise all the different types of information-providing materials that are given out to students or trainees, usually in connection with a taught lesson or programme of some sort. They include sets of notes (either complete or in skeleton form), tables, diagrams, maps and illustrative or extension material.

Assignment sheets: these include such things as problem sheets, reading lists, lab sheets, briefing sheets for projects and seminars, worksheets, etc. They can be used in practically all types of instructional situations.

Individualized study materials: these comprise all the different types of textual materials that are used in connection with individualized learning. They include study guides, structured notes, textual programmed materials and textual support materials for mediated learning systems.

Resource materials for group exercises: these comprise all the various printed and duplicated materials that are used in connection with group learning exercises. They include background reading material, briefing material, role sheets, instruction sheets, data sheets, and so on.

Non-Projected Display Materials

As its name suggests, this category includes all visual display materials that can be shown to a class, small group or individual student without the use of an optical or electronic projector of any sort. It includes a number of the most basic — and most useful — visual aids that are available to teachers and trainers, some of the more important of which are listed below.

Chalkboard displays: displays that are written, printed or drawn on a dark-coloured surface using chalk; still one of the most widely used of all visual aids, despite the fact that practically everything that can be done using a chalkboard can be done more easily, less messily, and (in most cases) more effectively using the overhead projector. Probably they are most useful for displaying impromptu 'signposts', notes and diagrams during a taught lesson and for working through calculations and similar exercises in front of a class.

Markerboard displays: displays that are written, printed or drawn on a light-coloured surface using felt pens or other wet markers of some sort. These can be used in the same ways as chalkboard displays and have the advantage of being less messy and offering a wider range of colours; also a markerboard can double up as a projection screen if necessary.

Feltboard displays: movable displays that are produced by sticking shapes cut out of or backed with felt or some similar material to a board covered with felt, or to a sheet of felt pinned on to a wall. This is a comparatively cheap, highly portable and extremely useful display technique, especially in situations that require the movement or re-arrangement of pieces (demonstrating table settings, carrying out sports coaching, etc).

Hook-and-loop board displays: similar to feltboard displays, except that the backing material on the display items possesses large numbers of tiny hooks that engage loops on the surface of the display board. These are suitable for displaying heavier items than feltboards.

Magnetic board displays: displays consisting of items that are made of or backed with magnetic material or fitted with small magnets so that they stick to a ferromagnetic display board. These can be used in much the same way as feltboard and hook-and-loop displays.

Flipchart displays: large sheets or paper hung from an easel of some sort so that they can be flipped forwards or backwards in order to reveal the information on a particular sheet or produce a fresh blank sheet on which impromptu information can be written or drawn.

Charts and wallcharts: large sheets of paper, carrying pre-prepared textual and/or graphical and/or pictorial information. Such charts can either be used to display information during the course of a lesson or can be pinned to the wall of a classroom in order to be studied by the students in their own time. Wallcharts, in particular, can be extremely useful for providing supplementary material or acting as a permanent *aide-mémoire* or reference system for learners (eg the periodic tables of the elements that are prominently displayed in practically all chemistry classrooms).

Posters: similar to wallcharts, but generally containing less information — often simply a single dramatic image. They are useful for creating atmosphere in a classroom.

Photographic prints: enlarged prints made from photographic negatives may be incorporated into textual materials, wallcharts, etc and, in linked sequences with suitable captions, can form a useful instructional medium in their own right. Such sequences are particularly suitable for use in programmes designed for individual study.

Mobiles: systems of two- or three-dimensional objects that are hung from the roof of a class by thread, thus producing a visually attractive display whose

	shape is constantly changing due to air currents. These are particularly useful for creating interest among younger children.
Models:	useful in cases where three-dimensional representation is necessary (eg crystal structures, animal skeletons, etc) or where movement has to be demonstrated.
Dioramas:	static displays that combine a three-dimensional foreground (eg a model landscape of some sort) with a two-dimensional background, thus creating an aura of solidity and realism.
Realia:	displays of real items (eg geological or biological specimens) as opposed to models or representations thereof. These are extremely useful if such materials are readily available and easily displayed.

Still Projected Display Materials

This category includes all visual display materials which do not incorporate movement and which require an optical projector of some sort in order to show them to a class or group or enable them to be studied by an individual learner. It again includes some of the most useful visual aids that are available to teachers, instructors and trainers, the most important of which are listed below.

Overhead projector transparencies and similar materials:	textual or graphical images on large acetate sheets that can either be displayed to a class or group using an overhead projector or viewed by individuals or small groups using a light box of some sort. These are probably the most useful and versatile visual aid that can be used to support mass instruction methods in the modern classroom, as we will see later.
Slides:	single frames of 35 mm photographic film mounted in cardboard, plastic or metal binders, often between twin sheets of glass (compact slides) or larger images roughly 3¼ inches square (lantern slides — now largely obsolete). These are one of the most useful methods of displaying photographic or graphic images to a class, small group or individual student using a suitable front or back projector or viewer — either singly or in linked sequences.
Filmstrips:	these are simply strips of 35 mm film carrying linked sequences of positive images, each usually

half the size of a standard 35 mm frame (half-frame or single-frame filmstrips) but sometimes the full size (full-frame or double-frame film-strips). They are a convenient and, when purchased commercially, comparatively cheap alternative to slide sequences and can be used in much the same ways, using suitable filmstrip projectors or viewers, for display or study.

Microforms: microform is a general term for any medium that is used to carry micro-images, ie photographically reduced images of pages of text, graphic materials, etc. The most common types are microfilms (rolls or strips of photographic film carrying a linear sequence of such images), microfiches (transparent sheets of photographic film carrying a matrix of such images) and microcards (opaque sheets carrying similar matrices of micro-images). All such microforms can be used to carry the frames of instructional programmes (eg programmed learning sequences), to act as highly compact databanks, etc, and can be studied using special magnifying viewers or projectors.

Audio Materials

This category includes all the various systems whereby straightforward audio signals can be played to or listened to by a class, group or individual. It includes a number of extremely useful — albeit often neglected — instructional aids, some of the most important of which are described below.

Radio broadcasts: educational radio broadcasts constitute an extremely useful free resource for teachers and trainers and, although they are often difficult to incorporate into the timetable if listened to at the time they are actually transmitted, this can easily be overcome by recording them for later playback. Note, however, that it is only certain designated educational broadcasts that can be so used without infringing the copyright laws.

Gramophone records: recordings of music, plays, etc on gramophone records constitute a relatively inexpensive and readily available instructional resource in certain subject areas. They are suitable both for playing to a class or group and for private listening by individuals, although they are not so convenient to store, handle or use as tape cassettes.

Audiotapes: audio material recorded on open-reel tape or tape cassette constitutes one of the most useful resources at the disposal of the modern teacher or trainer, and can be used in a wide range of instructional situations, either on its own or in conjunction with visual materials of some sort.

Linked Audio and Still Visual Materials

This is the first of the three classes in which audio and visual materials are combined to form integrated instructional systems and includes a number of media that are particularly suitable for use in individualized instruction. Some of the most commonly used systems are listed below.

Tape-slide programmes: audiotape recordings (usually on compact cassettes) synchronized with linked sequences of slides constitute one of the most useful and commonly used integrated audiovisual media. They can be used in a wide range of instructional situations, particularly individualized instruction.

Tape-photograph programmes: these are basically the same as tape-slide programmes, except that sequences of photographic prints are used instead of sequences of slides. Their range of applications is not as great, however, being largely restricted to individualized learning situations.

Filmstrips with sound: these are simply filmstrips that have an accompanying sound commentary, usually on a compact tape cassette. They can be used in much the same way as tape-slide programmes.

Radio-vision programmes: this is a technique pioneered by the British Broadcasting Corporation whereby still filmstrips are produced to accompany educational radio programmes. The filmstrips can either be shown to a class during the actual broadcast or used with a recording of the programme.

Tape-text: combinations of printed or duplicated materials with audio recordings constitute an extremely useful individualized instruction technique. The audio component can either be carried on a separate audiotape (usually a compact cassette) or carried on a special strip or sheet that is incorporated in the medium that carries the text; the latter systems (known as audiocards, audio-pages, talking pages, etc) require specialized equipment to use them.

Tape-model, tape realia, etc:	combinations of audiotapes (usually compact cassettes and other still visual display materials such as the three-dimensional models, collections of realia (eg geological and biological specimens) and microscope slides. Such hybrid systems can prove extremely useful vehicles for individualized instruction, as we will see in Chapter 6.

Cine and Video Materials

This class includes all media that enable audio signals to be combined with *moving* visual sequences, thus enabling a further dimension to be added to integrated audiovisual presentations. The main systems that are currently available are as follows.

Cine films:	such films have been in regular use in education and training for many years, and are available in a number of formats. The most commonly-used type is probably 16 mm, although 8 mm and super 8 mm films are also widely used, since they are much cheaper to make and show.
Loop films:	these consist of loops of cine film (usually 8 mm) mounted in special cartridges that enable them to be shown or viewed continuously using a custom-designed projector or viewer. Such loop films are ideal for teaching single concepts that require movement to demonstrate them to full advantage and, although they do not normally have an accompanying sound commentary, this can easily be added using a separate sound system.
Tape-film programmes:	these are highly sophisticated integrated systems that enable audio material to be combined with sequences of still and moving pictures. Most systems of this type use separate cassettes or cartridges to carry the audio and video components, and obviously require specialized equipment to show or view them.
Television broadcasts:	as in the case of educational radio broadcasts, educational television broadcasts constitute an extremely useful free resource for teachers and trainers. Like the former, they are not usually transmitted at convenient times but, thanks to the development of relatively cheap videorecorders, this limitation can now be easily overcome.

Readers should again note, however, that it is only certain designated educational television programmes that can legally be recorded for subsequent educational use, and that an appropriate licence is usually required even for this.

Videotape recordings: television sequences or programmes recorded on videotape now contribute one of the most useful and powerful instructional media at the disposal of teachers and trainers, and can be used in a wide range of teaching/learning situations as we will see later.

Videodisc recordings: although not yet as widely used as videotapes and videocassettes, videodiscs (in which the signal is recorded optically or electronically on the surface of a special disc, in the form of a spiral track similar to that on a gramophone record) have tremendous potential in education and training as we will see in Chapter 8.

Computer-Mediated Materials

This final category includes all the various materials that require a computer of some sort to enable them to be displayed, studied or used. Arguably, the computer constitutes the most important single resource ever to become available to teachers and trainers since the invention of the printing press and may well have a similar revolutionary effect on the way education and training are carried out, bringing about the massive shift from conventional expository teaching to mediated individualized learning that some commentators are currently predicting (see, for example, Hawkridge's book *New Information Technology in Education*). Whether or not this happens, there is no doubt that appropriate use of computers can be of tremendous assistance to the practising teacher or trainer. Some of the main types of computer-mediated systems are listed below.

'Number crunching' and data-processing packages: one of the most obvious uses of the computer in education and training is as a 'super-calculator' or data processor. It is now possible to acquire or produce software packages that enable virtually any calculation or data-processing task to be carried out automatically on the computer and, when appropriately used, such packages can be of tremendous help to both teachers and learners.

'Substitute tutor' packages: another obvious use of the computer is as a vehicle for administering individualized learning, since it has the potential to provide a degree of

interaction and feedback that no other system possesses. Thus 'substitute tutor' computer-based learning packages seem certain to become one of the most important tools available to teachers and trainers.

'Substitute laboratory' packages: a third important instructional application of the computer is as a vehicle for providing, through computer-based simulations, access to a far wider range of educational and training experiences than has ever been possible before. Again, such 'substitute laboratory' packages seem certain to become increasingly important tools for teachers and trainers of all types.

Database systems: as well as being used to process information, the computer can be used to store it and to help retrieve it when required. Thus teachers and trainers can now use computers to create databases that can be used in a whole range of instructional situations.

Computer-managed learning systems: a fifth major application of computers in education and training is their use in an administrative or managerial role, eg in the overall administration of the system, timetable planning, budgetary control, and the management of the actual teaching/learning process. Here again, software packages that enable these various things to be done are likely to become increasingly widely used.

Interactive video systems: such systems, which probably constitute the most powerful and potentially the most useful mediated instruction system yet developed, use a computer to gain access to video material stored in a random-access videorecorder in the context of a fully interactive computer-based learning programme. At the time of writing, however, it is uncertain whether they will ever become available at a cost that will enable them to be used in anything other than highly specialized training situations (eg by the armed forces and large industrial firms).

A summary of the main characteristics of all these various materials, considered from the point of view of the user and would-be producer, is given in Figure 1.2 on pages 26 and 27.

Type of materials	Instructional mode(s) for which materials are most suitable	Can materials be produced on-site by teachers and trainers?
Printed and duplicated materials	All modes	Yes
Chalkboard and marker-board displays	Mass instruction; group learning	Yes
Feltboard and similar materials	Mass instruction; group learning	Yes
Magnetic board materials	Mass instruction; group learning	Yes
Flipchart displays	Mass instruction; group learning	Yes
Wallcharts and posters	Mass instruction; group learning	Yes
Photographic prints	Mass instruction; group learning	Yes
Mobiles, models, etc	All modes	Yes
Realia	All modes	Yes
OHP transparencies	Mass instruction; group learning	Yes
Slides	All modes	Yes, but technical support may be needed
Filmstrips	All modes	Not easily
Microforms	Individualized instruction	Not easily
Radio programmes	All modes	Not without professional support
Gramophone records	All modes	No
Audiotapes	All modes	Yes
Tape-slide programmes	All modes, especially individualized instruction	Yes, but technical support may be needed
Tape-photo programmes	All modes, especially individualized instruction	Yes, but technical support may be needed
Sound filmstrips	All modes	Not easily
Radio-vision programmes	All modes	Not without professional support
Tape-text programmes	Individualized instruction	Yes
Tape-model and similar materials	Individualized instruction	Yes
Cine films	Mass instruction; group learning	Yes, but external processing required
Loop films	All modes	Yes, but external support required
Tape-film programmes	All modes, especially individualized instruction	Yes, but external support required
TV broadcast programmes	All modes	Not without professional support
Video materials (on videotape)	All modes	Yes, but technical support may be needed
Video materials (on videodisc)	All modes	No
Conventional CBL materials	All modes, especially individualized instruction	Yes
Interactive video materials	All modes, especially individualized instruction	Only if specialized facilities are available

Figure 1.2 *Summary of characteristics of different instructional materials*

Does production of materials require any specialized skill(s) other than instructional design skills?	Does production of materials require any specialized equipment?	Is any specialized equipment needed to use the materials?
Basic graphic skills	Printing or duplicating equipment	No
Basic graphic skills	Chalkboard or markerboard	Chalkboard or markerboard
Basic graphic and craft skills	No	Suitable display surface
Basic graphic and craft skills	No	Suitable display surface
Basic graphic skills	No	Suitable support system
Basic graphic skills	Not necessarily	No
Basic photographic skills	Appropriate photographic equipment	No
Appropriate craft skills	Not necessarily	No
No	No	No
Basic graphic skills	No	Projector and screen, or light box
Basic photographic and graphic skills	Appropriate photographic equip-equipment	Projector and screen, or viewer
Specialized photographic skills	Appropriate photographic equipment	Projector and screen, or viewer
Appropriate photographic skills	Appropriate photographic equipment	Suitable viewer
Professional production skills	Studio equipment	Radio receiver
External support required	Studio and manufacturing equipment	Record player
Basic recording and editing skills	Basic recording and editing equipment	Audiotape player
As for slides and audiotapes	As for slides and audiotapes	Audiotape player and projector or viewer
As for photographs and audiotapes	As for photographs and audiotapes	Audiotape player
As for filmstrips and audiotapes	As for filmstrips and audiotapes	As for filmstrips and audiotapes
Professional production skills	As for filmstrips and radio	As for filmstrips and radio
As for textual materials and audiotapes	As for textual materials and audiotapes	Audiotape player
As for models, etc and audiotapes	As for models, etc and audiotapes	Audiotape player
Basic cine production skills	Cine camera and sound equipment	Suitable cine projector and screen
External support required	Cine camera and special equipment	Special projector or viewer
As for cine films, slides and audiotapes	Special equipment required	Special projector/player
Professional production skills	TV studio facilities	TV receiver
Basic TV production skills	Basic video production facilities	Videotape player and TV monitor
External support required	Highly specialized equipment	Videodisc player and TV monitor
Basic programming skills*	Access to suitable computer or authoring system	Suitable computer
Programming skills;* video production skills	Video production facilities; CBL authoring and interface facilities	Computer, random-access videorecorder, TV monitor

*Not needed if authoring system used

Selecting Suitable Materials for Specific Purposes

Let us now consider some of the factors that should be taken into consideration by a practising teacher or trainer when choosing materials for some specific instructional purpose. In many cases, such selection is made purely on a basis of personal preference and availability, with little or no thought being given to the suitability of the materials for helping to achieve the desired instructional objectives. Inevitably this often leads to the use of inappropriate materials, with a resulting reduction in the effectiveness of the instructional process.

A large amount of basic research has been carried out on the relative effectiveness of different types of materials in different instructional situations. This shows that most media can perform most instructional functions to a certain extent, but that some are better at doing certain things than others, with no single medium being best for all purposes. Thus it is possible to adopt what is at least a semi-objective approach to the selection of instructional materials, based on consideration of the particular instructional strategy that is to be employed, the specific tactical methods to be used within that strategy, and the characteristics of the materials that can be used to support or implement these methods. Using such an approach, I have developed the algorithm given in Figure 1.3, which I hope readers will find helpful. This should be

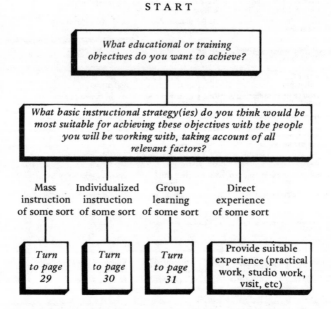

Figure 1.3 **Algorithm for selection of instructional materials**

START

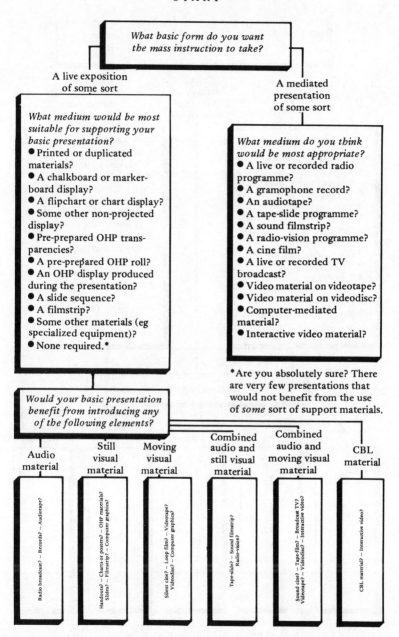

What basic form do you want
the mass instruction to take?

A live exposition
of some sort

A mediated
presentation
of some sort

What medium would be most
suitable for supporting your
basic presentation?
● Printed or duplicated
materials?
● A chalkboard or marker-
board display?
● A flipchart or chart display?
● Some other non-projected
display?
● Pre-prepared OHP trans-
parencies?
● A pre-prepared OHP roll?
● An OHP display produced
during the presentation?
● A slide sequence?
● A filmstrip?
● Some other materials (eg
specialized equipment)?
● None required.*

What medium do you think
would be most appropriate?
● A live or recorded radio
programme?
● A gramophone record?
● An audiotape?
● A tape-slide programme?
● A sound filmstrip?
● A radio-vision programme?
● A cine film?
● A live or recorded TV
broadcast?
● Video material on videotape?
● Video material on videodisc?
● Computer-mediated
material?
● Interactive video material?

*Are you absolutely sure? There
are very few presentations that
would not benefit from the use
of *some* sort of support materials.

Would your basic presentation
benefit from introducing any
of the following elements?

Audio
material

Still
visual
material

Moving
visual
material

Combined
audio and
still visual
material

Combined
audio and
moving visual
material

CBL
material

Radio broadcast? – Records? – Audiotape?

Handouts? – Charts or posters? – OHP materials?
Slides? – Filmstrip? – Computer graphics?

Silent cine? – Loop film? – Videotape?
Videodisc? – Computer graphics?

Tape-slide? – Sound filmstrip?
Radio-vision?

Sound cine? – Tape-film? – Broadcast TV?
Videotape? – Videodisc? – Interactive video?

CBL material? – Interactive video?

Figure 1.3 (continued) **Choosing materials for mass instruction**

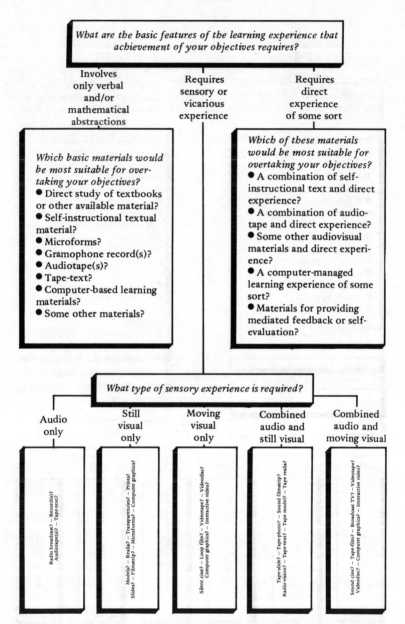

Figure 1.3 (continued) Choosing materials for individualized instruction

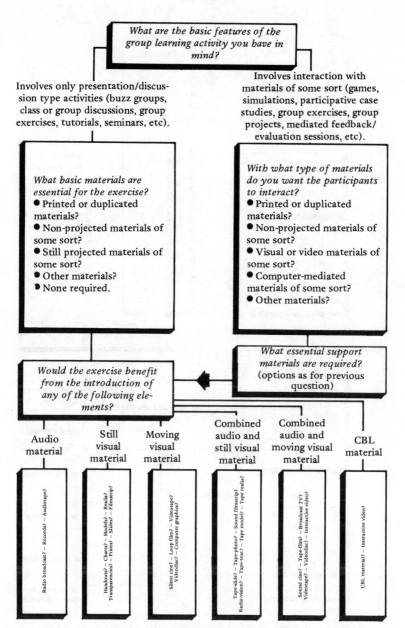

Figure 1.3 (continued) **Choosing materials for group learning**

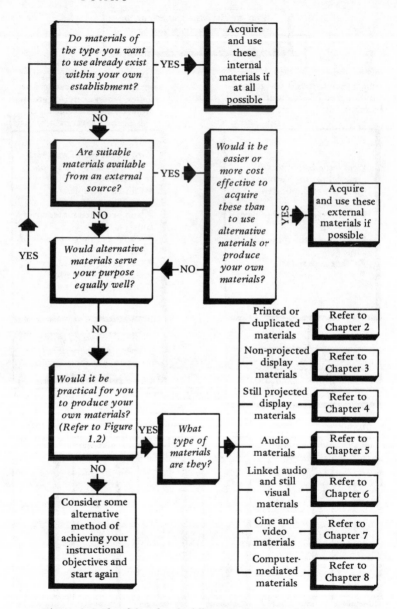

Figure 1.4 **Algorithm for deciding whether to produce your own instructional materials**

used to identify possible materials for achieving specific objectives, with the final selection being made after other factors such as availability or ease of production, availability of necessary equipment, cost, convenience and personal preference have been taken into account.

Deciding Whether to Produce your own Materials

Once a decision has been reached as to which materials will be needed to implement a chosen instructional scheme, it is obviously necessary to set about acquiring such materials or, if they are not readily available, determining whether it would be possible to produce them yourself. If the materials are *not* available from other sources, and it is *not* practicable to produce them yourself, then it will clearly be necessary to carry out a radical re-think regarding the method by which you are to achieve the particular set of instructional objectives that it was hoped they would help overtake. If you decide that you *do* want to try to produce the materials yourself, on the other hand, you should find detailed guidance on how to set about this task in one of the remaining seven chapters of this book. The algorithm in Figure 1.4 has been designed to help you decide which course of action to adopt in any particular set of circumstances; this should be completely self-explanatory.

Bibliography

Anderson, R H (1976) *Selecting and Developing Media for Instruction*. Van Nostrand Reinhold, Cincinnati.

Bretz, R (1971) *A Taxonomy of Communications Media*. Educational Technology Publications, Englewood Cliffs, New Jersey.

Elton, L R B (1977) Educational technology — today and tomorrow. In Hills, P and Gilbert, J (eds) *Aspects of Educational Technology XI*. Kogan Page, London.

Hawkridge, D (1982) *New Information Technology in Education*. Croom Helm, London.

Kemp, J E (1980) *Planning and Producing Audiovisual Materials*. Harper and Row, Publishers Inc, New York.

Kemp, J E (1971) Which medium? *Audiovisual Instruction*, **16** (December), pp. 32-6.

Levie, W H and Dickie, K E (1973) The analysis and application of media. In *Second Handbook of Research on Teaching*. Rand McNally, Chicago, pp 858-82.

Percival, F and Ellington, H I (1984) *A Handbook of Educational Technology*. Kogan Page, London/Nichols Publishing Company, New York.

Romiszowski, A J (1974) *The Selection and Use of Instructional Media*. Kogan Page, London.

Wittich, W A and Schuller, C F (1979) *Instructional Technology: Its Nature and Use*. Harper and Row, New York.

Chapter 2

How to Produce Printed and Duplicated Materials

Introduction

As we saw in Chapter 1, the various materials that can be prepared 'in-house' and run off in large numbers on a duplicator or printing machine constitute one of the most useful and versatile tools at the disposal of today's teachers and trainers. It is therefore appropriate that we should begin by discussing the preparation of such materials, despite the fact that they are, for some reason, often overlooked in texts on instructional media and audiovisual aids.

As in all subsequent chapters, we will start by taking a general look at how the materials can be used within the context of the different instructional strategies that were identified in Chapter 1. Next, we will carry out a detailed examination of how one should set about the task of planning and designing printed and duplicated materials, looking first at the basic principles that should underlie such design and then at the design of specific types of materials — handouts, worksheets, individualized learning materials, and so on. Finally, we will turn our attention to the various processes by which the materials can be mass produced, identifying the advantages and disadvantages of each process and offering guidance on which method to use in any particular situation.

How Printed and Duplicated Materials can be Used in Different Teaching/Learning Situations

In Chapter 1, we saw that there are three basic types of teaching/learning situations — mass instruction, individualized instruction and group learning — and that printed and duplicated materials can play a key, albeit different, role in each.

Mass Instruction

In the case of mass instruction, the role of printed and duplicated materials is essentially a supportive one, or: providing the teacher, instructor or trainer who is carrying out the instruction with tools that help him to achieve specific objectives or sub-sets thereof. Among the

most important of these tools are all the various forms of information —
providing handouts that can be given to the members of a class — sets
of notes, tables of data, copies of important diagrams, maps, and so on.
Appropriate use of such handouts can not only improve the effectiveness of the mass instruction process (by, for example, ensuring that
every member of the class — and not just those that are accomplished
note-takers or good graphic artists — ends the lesson with a decent set
of notes or a clear copy of a key diagram) but can also greatly increase
its efficiency (by, for example, reducing face-to-face contact time or
enabling a greater proportion of such time to be devoted to educa-
tionally useful activities such as exercises and discussions). At Robert
Gordon's Institute of Technology, for example, the electronic and
electrical engineering department made a policy decision in the early
1970s to cut down on formal class contact time by using handout
notes to provide basic information wherever possible. This certainly
did not reduce the effectiveness of its teaching (as measured by the
examination marks and classes of degree obtained by its students
before and after the change), but enabled it to make much more
efficient use of its teaching staff (as measured by the unit costs associated with the students on its various courses, which are now significantly
below those for most other departments teaching comparable subjects).
The change to handout notes also proved extremely popular with
students, who not only obtained better sets of notes than before but
also found that they had more time for private study because of their
shorter timetables.

The other main class of printed and duplicated materials that can be
used in mass instruction are assignment sheets of one form and another
— problem sheets, worksheets, lab sheets, and so on. As in the case of
handouts, appropriate use of such materials can greatly increase the
effectiveness of mass instruction of all types. Use of a well-designed
worksheet at an appropriate point in a taught lesson, for example, can
introduce a welcome participative element into what may otherwise be
a completely passive experience for the students, thus helping to maintain their concentration and interest. Recent research (see the paper by
Johnstone and Percival listed in the Bibliography) has shown that the
length of time for which a student can give his full attention to the task
of listening or taking notes (the so-called attention span) falls from
roughly 12-15 minutes at the start of a taught lesson or lecture to
around 3-5 minutes at the end, being interrupted by periodic attention
breaks (micro-sleeps) lasting for about 2 minutes. The occurrence of
such attention breaks can, however, be partly prevented by introducing
variety into the lesson, one of the most effective ways of doing this
being to get the students actively involved in a task of some sort.
Clearly, assignment sheets of various types are ideal for this purpose.

Individualized Instruction

As we have already seen, the role of instructional materials in individualized instruction is much more crucial to the learning process that is the case in mass instruction, since it is these materials that have to constitute the actual vehicle whereby the instruction process is carried out. In other words, self-instructional materials not only have to convey information to the learner, they also have to structure and control the process by which this information is presented to and assimilated by the learner. Such materials therefore need to be much more carefully designed than materials that are simply to be used to support mass instruction. Indeed, experience has shown that they can take up to ten times longer to produce.

Printed and duplicated materials can play three basic roles in individualized instruction. First, they can be used as the actual medium of instruction, eg in the form of structured notes, worksheets or programmed texts. If they are well-designed, such materials can enable pupils, students or trainees to master the basic facts and principles of a subject or topic at their own pace. Also, there is a considerable amount of evidence to suggest that the resulting degree of mastery is generally greater than that attained in the course of a conventional expository lesson, where the pace is dictated by the instructor.

Second, printed and duplicated materials can be used as a vehicle for structuring and controlling the process by which learners acquire information rather than as a means of conveying the information itself. Good examples of such materials are the various forms of study guide, which can be used to direct learners to relevant chapters (or parts thereof) in textbooks or instruct them on how to make optimum use of other individualized learning media such as tape-slide programmes, multi-media packages and home experiment kits.

Third, printed and duplicated materials can be used to support other individualized learning media. They can, for example, provide worksheets or diagnostic instruments for use in conjunction with audiovisual programmes or computer-based learning systems, provide illustrative or extension material, or give learners their own personal copies of key material for subsequent study or revision.

Group Learning

Unlike mass and individualized instruction, group learning is essentially a process-centred activity with the emphasis being on the interactions that take place between the people taking part rather than on the teaching or learning of facts, principles, etc. Thus, the role of any instructional materials that may be used in conjunction with a particular group-learning exercise is usually mainly supportive although, as we have seen, such materials can play a key part in making the exercise function smoothly.

Of the various media that can be used to support group-learning exercises, printed and duplicated materials are almost certainly the most versatile and important. They can, for example, be used to provide the basic resource materials on which the exercise is centred, provide the participants with instructions or guidance on how to carry out the exercise, and provide ancillary or illustrative material of various types. In most exercises that involve simulation or role play, for example, printed or duplicated materials are used to establish the basic scenario and brief the participants on their respective roles. They can also be used to provide things like worksheets, data sheets and background reading material, all of which are commonly used in group-learning exercises.

How to Plan and Design the Materials

Now that we have seen how printed and duplicated materials can be used in different types of teaching/learning situation, let us turn our attention to the way in which such materials should be planned and designed for specific purposes. We will begin by looking at some of the general principles that should underlie all such work of this type, then at how to tackle the design of particular types of printed and duplicated materials, looking in turn at handouts, worksheets, individualized study materials and resource materials for group-learning exercises.

Basic Principles Underlying the Design of Printed and Duplicated Materials

Although printed and duplicated teaching materials come in a wide range of types and vary greatly in format, layout, level and so on, I have found that it is possible to adopt a standard basic approach to their planning and design. This has the following three stages:

☐ Identifying the specific instructional role that you want the materials to play.
☐ Formulating a basic plan for the materials.
☐ Writing and designing the materials.

The full production process has, of course, a rather crucial fourth stage — producing the materials in whatever form and quantity are needed — but this will be considered separately later in the chapter. Let us now look at the three planning and design stages in greater detail.

IDENTIFYING THE INSTRUCTIONAL ROLE

This is, of course, the starting point in the planning and design of all teaching or training materials. It involves taking a detailed look at the learning objectives that you are trying to achieve, and identifying the specific areas where printed or duplicated material could help you do this within the overall context of the basic instructional strategy that you have decided to use.

FORMULATING A BASIC PLAN FOR THE MATERIALS

Identification of the role that you want the materials to play should be

of considerable assistance in the next stage of the design process —
formulating a basic plan for the materials. Indeed, in many cases, you
will find that the process is virtually automatic, with the basic design
parameters for the materials (their format, content and structure)
following logically from this role. I usually find that it is best to consider these three design parameters in turn, beginning by deciding what
sort of materials I want to use (a handout? a worksheet? a set of role
sheets? and so on), then deciding on the basic content, and finally
drawing up an outline structure. At each stage, I find that it is useful
to sketch my ideas out on scrap paper, a process that I find extremely
helpful in clarifying my thinking and eventually coming up with a
workable scheme. Needless to say this may well take several attempts.

WRITING THE MATERIALS
With some types of printed and duplicated materials, most of the
creative work is done at the basic design stage, with the actual writing
of the materials merely involving filling out these ideas and finalizing
the layout. With others, the writing stage is where the hard work starts,
involving many hours, days or even weeks of concentrated effort. This
is especially so in the case of lengthy materials such as linked series of
handout notes, suites of individualized instruction documents or integrated sets of resource materials for exercises of the game/simulation/
participative case study type. Obviously, it is vitally important to adopt
a systematic, disciplined approach to such work and readers should
find the following guidelines helpful in achieving this.

Matching the content to the design objectives and target population:
This is one of the most obvious things that a writer of instructional
materials has to get right if the materials are to achieve their design
objectives properly. Thus it is worthwhile spending some time thinking
about detailed content before embarking on the writing task. One way
of doing this is to ask yourselves the following three questions:

(a) What *must* the readers know after using the material?
(b) What, over and above (a), *should* the readers know after using the
    material?
(c) What, over and above (a) and (b), would it be useful if the readers
    knew after using the material?

Clearly, it is absolutely essential to include everything contained in
category (a), highly desirable to include everything in category (b) and
desirable to include as much of (c) as possible. Conversely, there is
absolutely no point in including anything that falls into none of the
three categories, unless it fulfils some other essential function.

Using an appropriate writing style: Adopting a writing style that is
appropriate both to the type of materials and the ability of the users is
one of the most difficult tasks facing every author. If one is only used
to writing formal reports or research papers for learned journals, for

example, it is never easy to change to the radically different style that is required for educational writing, particularly if the material is to be used with younger or less able learners. A number of authors offer hints on how this can be done, however, among the most useful of which are the 'Twelve hints for effective writing' given by Derek Rowntree in his book *Basically Branching* (see Bibliography):

1. Write as you talk.
2. Use the first person.
3. Use contradictions.
4. Talk directly to the reader.
5. Write about people, things and facts.
6. Use active verbs and personal subjects.
7. Use verbs rather than nouns and adjectives.
8. Use short sentences.
9. Use short paragraphs.
10. Use rhetorical questions.
11. Dramatize wherever possible.
12. Use illustrations, examples, case studies.

There are also a number of useful tests — both subjective and objective — that you can use to see whether your style needs to be improved in any way. The first, which is described in detail in *How to Write Self-Study Materials* by Roger Lewis (see Bibliography) involves reading something that you have written recently and asking yourself the following questions:

☐ Is my style pompous? formal? friendly? slapdash?
☐ Do I use too many clichés?
☐ Do I use more words than I need?
☐ Do I have favourite words and phrases that I over-use?
☐ Do I make frequent use of passive constructions? impersonal constructions? negatives?
☐ Are my sentences generally long or short?
☐ Do I use too many long words? abstract words? technical words?

If this self-evaluation process highlights any obvious faults in your writing style, you should make a deliberate effort to eliminate or mitigate them. If, for example, you find that you make too much use of the passive, check each paragraph that you write for a while and eliminate every passive verb; you will soon find that you make much less frequent use of such verbs.

A rather more objective test that can be used to determine whether the style of written educational material is suitable for the people who are to use it is the *Cloze Test*. This involves selecting a typical passage roughly 250 words long and, after a 35-word run-in, blanking out the next word and every tenth word thereafter until you have blanked out a total of 20. This blanking should be done by covering the words in question with suitable opaque material (eg plastic tape) that makes it impossible to read them. Once this has been done, select one (or, preferably, several) of the people in your target population and ask them to read the material. If they fail to provide the *correct* word or a *totally acceptable alternative* in at least 13 cases out of the 20, then the text is too difficult. If this is the case, modify the passage by simplifying the language and shortening the sentences.

Another objective method of determining whether the style of a text is appropriate to the people for whom it is intended is to calculate its *Modified Fog Index*, which gives a direct measure of the reading age of the material (ie the lowest age group by which the material is likely to be fully understood). This can be calculated as follows:

1. Choose a typical sample of the text, and work through a particular section, counting the words and sentences as you do so; stop at the end of the first sentence that takes you past 100 words. Calculate the average sentence length (asl) by dividing the total number of words by the number of sentences.
2. Work through the same sample again, counting the number of words with three or more syllables. Do not count words that are (a) capitalized, (b) combinations of short, easy words (like 'over-worked' or 'underground') or (c) verbs that only have three syllables because of endings like '-ed' and 'es' (eg 'deflated' and 'dismisses'). Calculate the percentage of hard words (%hw) in the passage by dividing the number of remaining words of three or more syllables by the total number of words and multiplying by 100.
3. Calculate the reading age of the passage using the formula:

Modified Fog Index = reading age (in years) = 0.4 (asl + %hw) + 5

If the average reading age of several typical passages in a given text turns out to be significantly greater than the age of the group for which it is intended, it again obviously requires modification by simplifying the language and shortening the sentences. Indeed, the reading level of educational material should, ideally, be well below the maximum level of difficulty with which the group can cope if they are not to find that the struggle simply to read the material inhibits mastery of the content. For this reason, any instructional material with a Modified Fog Index of over 20 is probably too difficult for any group — even highly literate university students — to cope with easily.

Two further points should be made regarding the Cloze Test and Modified Fog Index. First, both tests can only be used on passages of continuous prose, and are therefore unsuitable for checking the level of instructional material that consists of short sections (eg programmed texts) or is broken up with equations, tables, etc. Second, both tests tend to give an over-high indication of the reading age of material that contains a high percentage of scientific, technical or other specialized terms, and due allowance should therefore be made for this if necessary. Despite these limitations, however, the two tests constitute a reasonably accurate and useful method of checking the appropriateness of the level of textual material.

Adopting an efficient method of composing text: At this point, it would probably be useful to mention some of the different methods of working that it is possible for writers to adopt and, in particular, to make readers aware of the way in which recent developments in micro-electronics have made the task of composing textual materials very much easier than in the past.

There are four basic ways in which it is possible to compose textual material, three of which have been in use for many years. The first of these traditional methods is to write the material out in longhand — a slow and laborious method, but still the one that many authors (myself included) prefer. The second is to dictate the material into a tape recorder of some sort — a very efficient method indeed if you have the ability to 'think in paragraphs' and if the material that you are developing lends itself to this type of composition. The third is to work directly at a typewriter — a method that is used by many professional authors, since it is considerably quicker than the longhand method if you possess the necessary typing skills.

During the last few years, however, a totally new method of composing text has become available, namely, use of an electronic word processor. Such a device enables text to be created on the screen of a computer video display unit using a keyboard terminal and subsequently stored in the computer's memory system, from where it can be recalled or printed out in hard-copy form at any time. The main advantage of such a system over a conventional typewriter is that corrections and changes can be made to the text being worked on virtually instantaneously, thus enabling an author to produce perfect final copy as he works, without the need to type the same page over and over again if changes are required. Furthermore, the development of progressively cheaper word-processing equipment and software packages that enable inexpensive microcomputers to be converted into word processors means that more and more people are finding that they have access to such systems. Indeed, some commentators believe that virtually all instructional writing will be done on word processors within a few years. Such machines (they claim) will soon be just as common in school, colleges and training establishments as typewriters are today and, once\teachers and trainers find out how easy and convenient they are to use, they will (it is argued) abandon more traditional methods of composition for evermore. I must confess that I find this argument difficult to refute.

The importance of layout: Whatever type of material you are producing, the layout can be just as important as the content in determining whether it does its job effectively. Thus it is essential that you give a considerable amount of thought to how this content is to be presented to the reader. In the case of lengthy textual materials, for example, it is always an advantage to divide the content into clearly defined sections, and to use a systematic and logical labelling system to tell the reader what these sections are, indicate material of different types or degrees of importance, and so on. Appropriate use of things like different sizes, types and weights of print, underlining, boxing in of certain material, blank spaces and illustrations can also help to produce a clear, visually attractive and interesting layout. Some of these techniques are illustrated in Figure 2.2 — a good example of well laid-out instructional material.

Figure 2.1 Text being composed using a word processor; note the printer (on the extreme left) and the box of floppy discs (centre), which are used to store the completed text in coded form

How to Design Specific Types of Materials

Having dealt with some of the basic principles that should underlie the design of all types of printed and duplicated materials, let us now turn our attention to specific types of material and look at some typical examples.

HANDOUTS

These can be used for a wide range of purposes, and the detailed design of any particular handout will, of course, depend to a large extent on the exact role that it is to be required to play. Some commonly used types are listed below.

☐ Complete sets of notes on specific areas or topics, designed to be given to learners to save them from having to take notes themselves during lectures, training sessions, etc.

☐ Skeleton sets of notes, containing blank spaces that learners have to fill in themselves during a lesson of some sort. These can have educational advantages over complete notes in some situations, since they involve some participation on the part of the learner.

☐ Shorter documents (often only a single sheet) that are given out during a lesson to save the students from having to copy a complicated diagram, map, set of data, etc or to illustrate some specific point(s).

Two examples of handout material are given in Figures 2.2 and 2.3. Figure 2.2 shows one page from a booklet on domestic heating and insulation that was published by the Association for Science Education in 1980 as part of its sixth-form 'Science in Society' course package. The booklet was primarily designed to be used as the basic pupil resource document in a series of exercises based on the general theme of home heating and insulation, but can also be used as a straightforward handout on the subject since it is completely self-contained. It is in fact used in this way in several junior undergraduate courses in my own college, where the document was written for the ASE. The main reason why I have included it is that it provides a good example of the sort of style and layout that is ideal for educational documents of this nature. Note, in particular, how the use of a simple but effective illustration shows the pupil exactly what loft insulation is and how it is installed.

My second example is typical of the sort of single-sheet handout that can easily be prepared by any teacher, instructor or trainer for use within the context of a taught lesson. It is in fact one that I recently prepared myself for use in a second-year undergraduate course on atomic physics. The main purpose of this particular handout is to save the students from having to copy a rather complicated diagram into their notes, something that would not only take a considerable amount of time but which they would almost certainly get wrong in some way (the relative positions of the various horizontal lines, which represent electronic energy levels corresponding to different quantum numbers, are rather important).

I would like readers to note three things about this handout (do not worry about the content, which I assume is completely meaningless to all non-scientists). First, it took me less than half an hour to produce and required no professional graphic or secretarial support; nevertheless, it is just as effective as a highly polished, professionally produced equivalent in achieving its educational objectives. Second, note that this particular handout would not be of much use in an individualized learning situation, because it contains very little in the way of explanation of the physics involved; this is supplied by me when I 'talk round' the handout in the course of my lecture. Finally, note that I have used lower case printing rather than ordinary handwriting or upper case printing for the bulk of the textual content, since research has shown that this is by far the easiest form of text to read. Thus, anyone who is

3. METHODS OF IMPROVING THE INSULATION OF A HOUSE

The better a house is insulated, the less heat will be lost when the rooms are maintained at their design temperatures and the lower will be the running costs of a central heating system. The present cost of all forms of fuel is high, and is certain to become even greater because of inflation and diminishing reserves of primary energy sources such as oil and coal. It is therefore important to examine the various ways in which insulation can be improved. The advantages and disadvantages of each type of insulation are summarised below.

Loft insulation

In an average house, it is estimated that roughly 25% of the heat losses occur through the roof. This heat loss can generally be greatly reduced by laying some sort of insulating material (such as glass fibre quilting or a layer of expanded polystyrene pellets) between the joists in the loft.

Advantages	Disadvantages
(a) Installation involves little or no disturbance in the home.	(a) There may be some risk of condensation problems or of frost damage to pipes and tanks in colder roof spaces.
(b) An easy method for "do-it-yourself" householders.	
(c) A very effective insulation method for reducing heat losses in a bungalow or house of large roof area.	
(d) Installation is relatively inexpensive.	
(e) It is the only one of the three main insulation methods that can be moved to another house.	

Loft insulation

4

Figure 2.2 **A page from a handout booklet on domestic central heating and insulation designed for use at upper secondary level with Science in Society students**

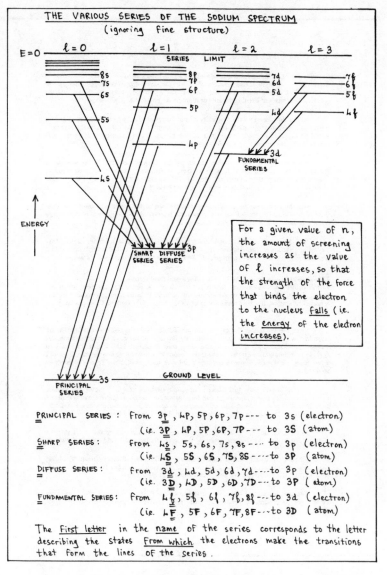

Figure 2.3 **A single-sheet handout designed for use during an undergraduate lecture on atomic physics**

4. PEAT-FIRED POWER STATION

Examination of technical feasibility of building a peat-fired station
Elaskay is fortunate in having a source of peat in the easily accessible Moor of Bogle 3 km south of Portian (see map). You may assume that a detailed survey has shown that the recoverable reserves of dried high-grade peat are of the order of 800 000 tonnes.

Let us now examine the feasibility of building peat-fired stations of the various sizes shown in row 1 of the Work Sheet opposite. The number of units of electricity that each would be expected to produce in a year is given in row 2, and the amounts of energy (MJ) that these figures represent are given in row 3. (1 kWh = 3.6 MJ).

But a peat-fired power station has an overall efficiency of 25%. So the amount of energy that each station would have to get from its peat supply each year is given in row 4. Since every tonne of peat contains roughly 9500 MJ of energy, we can calculate the number of tonnes of peat that each station would consume every year (row 5).

Use the figures for the annual fuel consumptions of the various stations to calculate the length of time for which Elaskay's recoverable reserves of 800 000 tonnes of peat would last if stations of different sizes were built (row 6).

Now assess the feasibility of building stations of different sizes, bearing in mind that a peat-fired station has an effective operational life of 25 years and it can only be justified economically if there is sufficient peat to keep it running throughout this period (row 7)

Examination of economic viability of building a peat-fired station
In this project, we will assume that it is the cost of the electricity produced which will largely decide which type of power station will be built. In order to calculate this figure for a peat-fired station, it is first necessary to know the costs of the station. These can be found as follows.

First, use the figures for capital cost per installed kW of generating capacity that are given in row 8 of your Work Sheet to calculate the capital cost of each station. (Note that the cost per installed kW falls as the size of the station increases; this is true for nearly all types of power station, and is one of the main reasons why Generating Boards generally build a few really big stations rather than a large number of small ones). Write down your answers to row 9.

A loan would have to be taken out to pay the full cost of building the station. Calculate the annual repayments on that loan, assuming that a low-interest loan is available such that the loan is repaid and the interest is covered by annual payments of £7.82 throughout the 25 year life of the station for every £100 borrowed (row 10).

Next, calculate the total annual cost of extracting, transporting and processing the peat needed to fuel the stations, assuming that every tonne used would cost £6 (row 11).

Finally, calculate the total annual costs (row 13) of the different stations by adding the annual repayments on capital cost (row 10), the annual extracting and processing costs (row 11) and the annual running and maintenance costs (row 12).

The cost per unit of electricity produced by the different stations (row 14) can now be obtained by dividing the total annual costs (row 13) by the annual electrical output (row 2).

6

Figure 2.4 **Case study on peat power from
Alternative Energy Project (text)**

WORK SHEET FOR PEAT POWER				
1.	Size of station (MW)	5	10	15	20
2.	Annual electrical output (million kWh units)	10	20	30	40
3.	Amount of energy this represents (million MJ)	36	72	108	144
4.	Amount of energy that has to be produced from combustion of fuel (million MJ)	144	288	432	576
5.	Annual fuel consumption (tonnes)	15 100	30 300	45 400	60 600
6.	Times for which fuel reserves would last (years)				
7.	Feasibility of building station with operational life of 25 years (yes/marginal/no)				
8.	Capital cost per installed kW (£)	600	550	525	500
9.	Capital cost of building station (£ million)				
10.	Annual repayments on capital cost (£)				
11.	Annual cost of extracting, transporting and drying peat (£)				
12.	Annual running and maintenance costs of station (£)	50 000	70 000	85 000	95 000
13.	Total annual operating costs of station (£)				
14.	Cost per unit of electricity generated (p)				

7

Figure 2.4 **Case study on peat power from
Alternative Energy Project (worksheet)**

planning to produce hand-written instructional materials of any type should try to develop a clear lower-case printing style; given a little practice, this can be produced almost as quickly as ordinary writing, and, in about all cases, is much more legible.

WORKSHEETS

These come in almost as many forms as handouts, and can be used in just as wide a range of instructional situations. Again the detailed design will depend to a great extent on the purpose for which the worksheet is intended. We can, however, distinguish between at least two basic types:

☐ Highly structured, 'convergent' worksheets, where the answers or other material that the learner has to fill in are largely (or completely) predetermined by the writer.
☐ More open-ended worksheets, where the responses are not nearly so circumscribed and allow the learner scope for divergent thinking or the exercise of creativity.

Both types can be used in all three of our basic classes of instructional situation (mass instruction, individualized instruction and group learning), although the former is probably the one that is best suited for individualized instruction, where the learning experience generally needs to be fairly tightly structured.

Typical examples of the two types of worksheet are given in Figures 2.4 and 2.5. The first (an example of a 'convergent' worksheet) is one of a set of five similar worksheets that are included in an interactive case study known as the *Alternative Energy Project* (again published by the Association for Science Education). This involves five small groups in carrying out independent feasibility studies into the possibility of generating electricity on the hypothetical Western Scottish island of 'Elaskay' by exploiting different alternative energy resources, after which the groups pool their findings and draw up a 50-year rolling programme for meeting Elaskay's future electricity needs. The worksheet is used in conjunction with the text on the facing page, with the two components (the text and the worksheet) together constituting a highly structured mini-case study into the feasibility of building peat-fired power stations of different sizes on the island — a case study that would, incidentally, be just as suitable for use in an individualized learning situation as in the small-group learning situation for which it was written.

The second example (a typical 'divergent' worksheet) is one that is used in another group learning exercise known as *Which Material?*. This was recently developed in RGIT for use in the new 'Foundation and General Level Science' courses that are currently being introduced into Scottish schools. The exercise is basically a very simple one, involving small groups trying to decide what would be the most suitable materials with which to manufacture different articles. Each group is allocated a different article (the frame of a chair, the casing of an electric plug, a power transmission cable, and so on) and has to try to think of four possible materials from which it could be made. The group then tries to identify the advantages and disadvantages of each material, and, on the basis of these, decides which material would be best. The solutions that the various groups come up with are then used as the basis of a class discussion.

As can be seen by comparing Figures 2.4 and 2.5, the two work-sheets are completely different in character, and are designed to give the users totally different types of learning experience. Examples of other types of worksheet can be found in *Worksheets and School Learning* (see Bibliography), an inexpensive booklet that is highly recommended to any schoolteacher who is interested in producing such items.

INDIVIDUALIZED LEARNING MATERIALS

As we saw earlier, materials that are intended for use in individualized instruction have to be much more carefully designed than most other types of instructional materials, because they have to control or manage the actual instruction process as well as supply the content. We also saw that printed and duplicated materials can play three basic roles in self-instructional systems:

1. They can constitute the actual vehicle by which the instruction takes place.
2. They can be used to structure and/or control or manage the instruction process, with the main instruction being carried out via other media (eg books or tape-slide programmes).
3. They can be used to support other individualized learning media by, for example, providing worksheets.

To deal in any depth with the subject of the design of self-instructional printed materials would require a complete book in itself, so I will not even attempt to do so here. (Readers who are interested in developing such materials are referred to two excellent (and inexpensive) introductory booklets on the subject — *How to Write Self-Study Materials* by Roger Lewis and *Programmed Learning: Writing a Programme* by Jacquetta Megarry; full details of both are given in the Bibliography.) Instead, I will simply show readers the opening section of one of the best examples of textual individualized learning material that I have so far come across — a linear programmed text, *Cheques*, developed by the Royal Bank of Scotland for use in training counter staff.

Possible material	Advantages	Disadvantages

WHICH MATERIAL?
Pupil Worksheet

Item to be manufactured

Recommended material

Figure 2.5 The pupil's worksheet from Which Material?

(The preliminary page)

To the student

1. As you read through these programmes you will require to think out, and on occasion write down, the answers to questions and problems.

2. The pages in this programme are divided into numbered sections known as frames. Some frames are presented in this format:

Commentary and question

— —

Answer to question

---

3. You cannot think out for yourself something that you have just read, and even the most honest eyes wander, so use a piece of paper to shield the answers at all times. Slide the paper down to the dashed line so that you can see everything above it; make your response and then compare it with the answer given.

4. At the end of each programme you are required to do a written test. The purpose of this is only to show both yourself and your accountant whether or not you have understood the subject matter, so do not worry about it.

5. If you have found difficulty understanding any of the material it may prove worthwhile to re-read the programme after an interval of a week or so.

Now proceed with the programme.

(The start of the programme proper)

Section 1 — Cheques

Technical details

1. Prior to going on to the cash you will undoubtedly have dealt with innumerable cheques in the bank whether this has been on the ledger or back desk. On the telling counter you will come to deal more closely with cheques. Frequently you will

---

Figure 2.6 **Part of a programmed text, on** *Cheques*, **designed for use in training bank employees**

be giving out cash against them, so you will require to know exactly what a cheque is and be able to analyse it for discrepancies. Remember, the bank may lose money if you give out cash indiscriminately, therefore you must be sure that the cheque is in order before cash is given out.

2. Let us then consider what kind of details we are looking for before cash can be given out.

There are various essentials which should be included on a cheque. Five of these essentials are highlighted on the specimen below.

These are as follows:

1. It should be in writing.
2. It must be signed by the drawer.
3. It must be drawn for a specified or certain sum of money.
4. It is dated.
5. It is payable to the order of a specified person (or to the bearer).

Have a look at the specimen cheque below and study these details as we will discuss them one at a time to see what they mean to us.

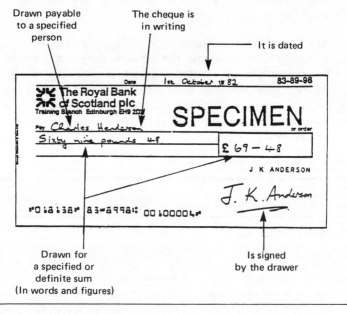

3. It should be in writing.

This means that the cheque may be made out in *any form* of

Figure 2.6 (continued)

writing, eg it may be in ink, typed, printed or handwritten.
Do you think that one drawn in pencil would be acceptable?

Yes

One drawn in pencil *would* be in order as it would still be in
writing.

Due to the ease, however, with which such cheques could be
altered by an unauthorised person, the banks *discourage*
customers from drawing them in *pencil*.

---

4. It must be signed by the drawer.
   This is straightforward. The cheque is not the order of the
   customer until it is signed by him or by someone duly
   authorised to do so on his behalf.

---

5. It must be drawn for a specified or certain sum in money.
   The sum on a cheque must be stated with certainty. You
   could not have a cheque 'pay John Brown £15 or £20'. The
   sum to be paid in this case is not certain, ie it is not definite.
   The amount should be in writing and in figures and the two
   should agree. If they differ the bank cannot ascertain which
   amount is to be paid, and in such cases, the cheque should
   not be paid until the discrepancy is put right by the drawer.
   The amount should thus be ascertainable with certainty.

---

6. It is dated.
   The date on a cheque is one point which must be looked at
   prior to cashing or paying it. It may be that it bears no date
   and although the Cheques Act would appear to say that a
   bank, as holder of the cheque, could fill in the date, banks
   do not generally do so, as it might be argued later by the
   drawer that he did not wish the cheque to be paid at that
   time. The cheque must bear a date before it is cashed. There
   is nothing to prevent the payee or holder filling in the date.

---

7. A cheque may also be 'post-dated' or 'ante-dated'.
   A post-dated one is where the date inserted is in advance of
   the date of issue. It is ante-dated when the date is prior to the
   issue. There is nothing which prevents you from cashing an
   ante-dated cheque so long as the cheque is not 'stale', ie
   out-of-date. Now what do we mean by that?
   Well, a cheque is said to be 'stale' or out-of-date when it has
   been in circulation for 'an unreasonable length of time'. But
   what is an unreasonable length of time? There is nothing in

Figure 2.6 (continued)

the statute book to guide the bank here but it is generally taken in practice that this means six months or more. A cheque thus bearing a date six months or more prior to the current date is considered stale and should not be cashed, unless the drawer alters the date and adds his initials.

8. It is payable to the order of a specified person or to bearer. If you were presented with a cheque for cashing, the payee (ie the person or parties to whom the sum is to be paid) must be named specifically, and one must be in no doubt as to whom the money is to be paid.
   Alternatively, the cheque may be drawn payable to 'bearer' — although this practice is rare — which indicates that the bearer or holder of the cheque may be given the cash. As you can see, such a practice could be dangerous as a thief could quite easily cash the cheque if he were the holder.

9. Now, with the specimen below examine it and then write down the essentials which are included in it. If there is any discrepancy in the cheque or any essential missing, state what.

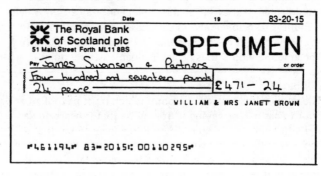

1. It is in writing.
2. It is payable to a specified person.
   Essentials Required:
1. It is not dated.
2. It is not for a certain sum, as the amounts differ (£ in figures say 471; words say 417).
3. It is not signed.

and so on

Figure 2.6 (continued)

GROUP LEARNING MATERIALS

As in the case of mass instruction and individualized instruction, printed and duplicated materials are capable of playing a wide variety of roles in group learning situations. Again, the detailed design of the materials depends to a large extent on the exact nature of this role. Some of the most commonly used types are listed below:

☐ Materials providing instructions or guidance on how to carry out or run an exercise (instruction sheets for participants, organizer's guides, and so on).
☐ Basic resource materials for use in the exercise (role sheets, background information documents, data sheets, worksheets, and so on).
☐ Ancillary, illustrative and extension materials of various types.

When designing the resource materials for a group-learning exercise, it is important to ensure that each item is capable of fulfilling its own specific function, fits into the general context of the exercise and is consistent with all the other materials in the package. This will almost certainly require. a certain amount of 'tuning', ie revising or amending particular items as the work progresses in order to produce a self-consistent, balanced package. Readers who are interested in making use of group-learning techniques in their work, and who wish to receive further guidance on how to design the necessary resource materials, are referred to two books that I have written on the subject with Eric Addinall and Fred Percival – *A Handbook of Game Design* and *Case Studies in Game Design* (see Bibliography). These cover the design of virtually all the different types of printed and duplicated materials that can be used in group-learning exercises, with the latter containing large numbers of illustrative examples of such materials.

A typical example of a resource document designed for use in a group-learning exercise – in this case, a structured debate on the safety and social acceptability of nuclear power – is given in Figure 2.7. This particular exercise forms the last of three projects in an educational package entitled *The Nuclear Debate* that was recently published by the Scottish Council for Educational Technology. The document shown is one of the 16 briefing sheets that are supplied to participants in the debate, and illustrates the three basic functions that such sheets should fulfil: (i) introducing the scenario of the exercise, (ii) telling the participant what his role will be, and (iii) providing any information specific to the role.

How to Produce Multiple Copies of the Materials

Having dealt at some length with the planning and design of printed and duplicated instructional materials, let us now turn our attention to the various ways in which it is possible to produce multiple copies of such materials for use by a class, group or set of individual learners. Basically, there are four practical methods by which this can be done within a

The Nuclear Debate   Briefing Sheet 3.1

Introduction
The object of Project 3 of *The Nuclear Debate* is to examine the question
of whether nuclear power is socially and environmentally acceptable in an
open society such as Britain. This will involve trying to answer the following
questions:

  (i) Are workers in the nuclear power industry subjected to unacceptably
       high accident and/or health risks?
 (ii) Does the nuclear power industry constitute an unacceptable hazard to
       the health and safety of the general public?
(iii) Does nuclear power constitute an unacceptable genetic hazard to the
       human race?
 (iv) Does nuclear power constitute an unacceptable political hazard
       because it is likely to lead to a reduction in personal freedom and to
       the spread of nuclear weapons?

The exercise will take the form of a structured debate in which each of the
above issues will be discussed in turn.

Your role in the exercise
You have been given the task of speaking **against** nuclear power in stage (i)
of the debate (discussion of the danger to workers in the nuclear power
industry). To help you do so, you have been provided with information
about the radiation safety limits that are currently in operation. Use this
to prepare as strong a case as possible. An overhead projector and screen
will be available during the debate, and it is strongly recommended that
you make use of the blank acetate sheets and felt pens with which you
have been provided to prepare visual materials to support your arguments
(eg tables).

Your information
1. It has long been recognized that ionizing radiation is dangerous, and
   potentially lethal. Many of the early scientific workers on radioactivity,
   X-rays, etc subsequently died of various forms of cancer such as
   leukaemia that were directly attributed to the radiation to which they
   had been exposed (Madame Curie, for example). Also, radioactive
   materials may be ingested or inhaled, thus giving rise to continuous
   long-term exposure to radiation.
2. Since 1910, as evidence increasingly linked cancer to exposure to radiation, the permissible exposure limits have been progressively lowered.
   In the 1930s, medical reports showed that workers in the uranium
   mining industry were subjected to well above average cancer risks.
   Later, during the 1950s, it was shown that *even small* doses of radiation
   cause damage to the basic genetic materials shared by animals and men.
   Small doses of X-rays given to children while in their mother's womb,
   for example, were found to increase greatly the risk that they would
   subsequently develop leukaemia. Also, the effects of exposure to
   radiation never disappear. In Japan, for example, over 100 people still
   die *every year* because of the radiation that they were exposed to as a
   result of the atom bombs dropped on Hiroshima and Nagasaki. All the
   evidence suggests that there is *no such thing as a 'safe' dose of radiation*.
   Any dose, however small, is potentially harmful. (See Introductory

Figure 2.7 **One of the briefing sheets for participants in
Project 3 of 'The Nuclear Debate'**

Booklet for further information about the harmful effects of ionizing radiation.)

3. Despite all this evidence, radiation safety levels are still set at an unacceptably high level, namely 5 rems per year for workers in the nuclear power industry, and 0.5 rems per year for members of the general public (see the Introductory Booklet for the definition of the rem). Thus, workers in the nuclear power industry are liable to be subjected to *over 30 times the dose that they receive from natural sources* (roughly 140-180 millirems per annum, depending on where they live).

4. As an illustration of the unacceptably high nature of these limits, consider the situation at Windscale, where the workforce is subjected to a total of roughly 10,000 man rems of radiation *every year.** It has been estimated that this will result in at least one cancer death per decade for every year of exposure at this level. Thus a large number of Windscale workers have already been condemned to premature death due to cancer.

* The total dose sustained by the workforce at Windscale was 12,000 man rems in 1976 and 8,000 man rems in 1979.

Figure 2.7 (continued)

school, college or training establishment — photocopying, hectographic duplication, stencil duplicating and small offset lithographic printing. We will therefore look at each of these in turn, explaining how they work and identifying their main strengths and weaknesses, after which we will discuss how to set about choosing which method to use in a particular situation.

Photocopying

The generic term 'photocopying' covers a wide range of different processes, but they all make use of light of some sort to produce a copy (or multiple copies) of an original document. Possibly the greatest advantage of this method is that the original requires no special preparation, since virtually any type of document (a typed or handwritten sheet, a sheet carrying graphic information, a page in a magazine or book, or even a photograph) can be copied on most modern machines.

The principle on which the photocopiers that are most useful for making multiple copies operate involves making use of electrostatic forces to transfer pigmented powder of some sort to the parts of the copy paper on which an image is to be produced and then using heat to fuse this powder to the surface of the paper in order to make the image permanent. Two main processes are used: direct electrostatic (where the pigment is deposited directly on to the surface of the copy paper) and transfer electrostatic (where the pigment is first deposited on the photo-sensitive surface of a rotating drum and then transferred on to the copy paper). Transfer electrostatic photocopiers have two considerable advantages over direct electrostatic machines. First, they use ordinary paper as copy paper, as opposed to the special (and more expensive) zinc oxide-coated paper that is needed for direct electro-static machines. Second, they can be made to operate much faster than direct machines, a considerable advantage when it comes to producing multiple copies. For these reasons, most multiple photocopying is now done on transfer electrostatic machines, which are becoming increas-ingly versatile and sophisticated every year. A typical medium-sized machine of this type is shown in Figure 2.8. This is housed in the central library on my college's main campus, and is extensively used by academic staff to run off multiple copies of handouts and other teaching materials. It can produce collated sets of multiple-page docu-ments — a great time saver for busy staff. An even larger, faster and more sophisticated machine of similar type is housed in our college's central reprographic unit, which handles all the large jobs and long print runs. There is, of course, no limit on the number of copies that can be produced from a given original.

One slight disadvantage of the use of photocopiers to run off copies of hand-prepared materials is that certain colours of ink do not copy well (or at all) on some machines. Thus, when preparing the masters of such materials, care should be taken to employ colours that will repro-duce on the machine to be used.

Figure 2.8 **A typical medium-sized electrostatic photocopier**

Hectographic Duplicating

This method, which is also known as spirit duplicating or Banda (from the trade name of one of the leading manufacturers), is one of the simplest non-photographic methods of producing multiple copies of single-sheet material. It is also by far the easiest method of producing multi-colour copies.

PREPARING THE MASTER

Unlike photocopying, hectographic duplication involves preparing a special master copy (known as a hectograph master) of the material to be duplicated. This is done by typing, writing or drawing on a special sheet of plain glossy paper which is in contact with the dye side of the hectograph transfer sheet of the required colour. This is coated with a special type of aniline dye, some of which is transferred on to the underside of the master, where a reversed image of the original materials is produced. Multi-colour masters can be produced by using different coloured master sheets, one after the other.

Hints on hectograph master preparation: If the master is being typed:

- [ ] Use a standard-sized typewriter rather than a light, portable machine.
- [ ] Set the typewriter to stencil or remove the ribbon.
- [ ] Use the special backing sheet supplied in the box of transfer sheets.

If the master is being prepared by hand:

- [ ] Lightly sketch out the material on the matt side of the master sheet before inserting the master sheet.
- [ ] Place the master sheet and transfer sheet on a sheet of glass or similar hard, smooth surface during the actual preparation; use a fine ball point pen or stylus to write or draw on the material.
- [ ] Fill in any blocks of colour required by rubbing hard with a soft (B) pencil.

In both cases; leave a margin of at least 1 cm all round. To correct mistakes, first cover over with special paint or eraser, *or* cover the mistake with a small piece of clean master paper, *or* carefully scrape off the dye with a scalpel or razor blade. Then insert the correction using a fresh corner of transfer sheet.

RUNNING OFF MULTIPLE COPIES

This is done using a machine of the type shown in Figure 2.9.

The completed master is fixed to the master drum of the duplicating machine, dye side outwards. A carefully aligned stack of copy paper is placed in the input tray, and sheets are then pulled through the machine one by one by turning the handle (or, in the case of some machines, switching on the motor). As it passes through the machine, each sheet is first lightly moistened with spirit by means of a felt pad (hence the name spirit duplication), and is then pressed against the rotating master drum by a pressure roller. As the paper is pressed against the master, the moistened paper picks up a small amount of dye, thus producing a permanent image on its surface.

Since some of the dye on the master is used up every time a copy is made, each master can only be used to produce a limited number of copies — possibly as many as 200 when the purple dye is used and considerably fewer (perhaps only 100) with other colours. Also, the method does not give high-quality, high-definition copies (since the nature of the dye transfer process gives rise to some spreading and smudging) and can be messy for the user. Nevertheless, it is a quick, cheap and handy method that will probably remain in use for a long time.

Figure 2.9 **A hectograph duplicator**

Stencil Duplication

Like hectograph duplication, stencil duplication is also commonly referred to by the names of leading equipment manufacturers. Thus, in the UK, the name roneo is used, while in the USA, the corresponding name is mimeograph.

PREPARING THE MASTER

Again as in the case of hectograph duplication, stencil duplication involves preparing a special master — the stencil from which the process gets its name. This is made from a thin sheet of special porous paper coated with a waxy substance that is impervious to ink, the stencil being prepared by typing or otherwise breaking through the coating (eg by drawing or writing) in order to produce the required image.

Hints on stencil preparation: If the stencil is being typed (the easiest and most effective method):

☐ Use a standard-sized typewriter rather than a light portable machine.
☐ Set the typewriter to stencil or remove the ribbon.
☐ Insert a sheet of carbon paper between the stencil paper and the backing sheet in order to make the image clearly legible.

If the stencil is being prepared by hand:

☐ Lay the stencil (with backing sheet still attached) on a suitable hard surface — preferably a special stencil preparation board.
☐ Carefully write or draw on the material using a suitable stylus (or, if not available, a fine ball point pen), taking great care not to tear the stencil.

In both cases, keep within the guidelines shown on the stencil that correspond to the size of copy paper that is to be used.

Electronic stencil cutters, which make stencils from original documents in the form of single sheets, are also available but these are both slow and expensive to use.

To correct mistakes, cover the error with a thin layer of stencil correction fluid and, once this has dried, carefully re-type, re-write or re-draw the relevant material, making sure that the layer of dried correction fluid has been penetrated.

RUNNING OFF MULTIPLE COPIES

Stencil duplication involves squeezing ink through the holes in the impervious, waxy coating of the stencil on to porous copy paper, where it is absorbed into the surface to produce a permanent image once the ink has been allowed to dry. This is done using a machine of the type shown in Figure 2.10 — a machine that is in many ways similar to a hectograph duplicator.

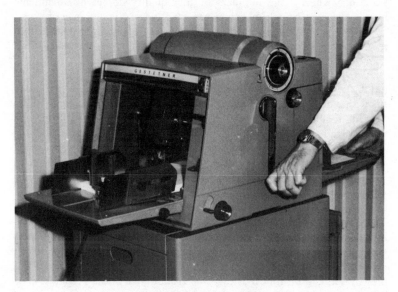

Figure 2.10 **A stencil duplicator**

To run off copies using a particular stencil, the thick paper backing sheet is removed and the stencil attached to the ink-drum, which is made of porous metal that allows the ink to ooze through from the inside to the outer surface, on to which the stencil is stuck (literally). Copies are then run off by turning the handle (or switching on the motor in the case of an electrically powered machine). This pulls sheets of copy paper through the machine one at a time, the sheets again being pressed against the rotating drum by means of a pressure roller. Since the ink on the completed copies may take a little time to dry, it is advisable to stack them in a dry, warm place for some time before use (a few hours is usually sufficient).

Stencil duplication has two advantages over hectograph duplication. First, it can be used to produce many more copies – several thousand, if the stencil is carefully handled and is cleaned and properly stored between print runs. (Special stencil storage boxes, in which the stencils are hung vertically by the cardboard tops to which they are attached, are used for this purpose.) Second, they can, if well prepared, produce a much sharper, better-quality image. Stencils are messy to use, however, and the ink is difficult to remove from hands and clothing.

Small Offset Litho Printing

The term 'small offset' is used to describe the small-scale offset lithographic machines that are now becoming increasingly widely used in situations where large numbers of high-quality copies of documents have to be made. Such machines are available in a wide range of types, sizes and prices, ranging from basic table-top machines that cost little more than a stencil duplicator to highly sophisticated presses that are comparable to those found in commercial printing firms.

PREPARING THE MASTER

Like the previous two duplication processes described, small offset printing required the preparation of a suitable master. These come in a wide range of types, catering for a variety of purposes – and budgets. The cheapest paper plates can cost less than the stencils used in stencil duplication, and can be used to produce similar numbers of copies – up to several thousand. More expensive metal plates produce better quality prints, and can be used to produce much larger numbers of copies – tens of thousands if need be. Both types of plates can be given their image either directly or via some plate-making process. Direct methods include typing (using a special greasy lithographic ribbon in the typewriter), writing or drawing with a special ballpoint pen, or painting. Provided that greasy finger marks are kept off the surface, such direct preparation can be almost as easy and trouble-free as the preparation of hectograph masters. At the other end of the scale, plates for the highest quality work – including full three-colour printing – can be made using conventional photo-litho methods similar to those used by commercial printing organizations. Basically this involves first making a film negative of the material to be printed, and transferred the image to a light-sensitive lithographic plate which is then developed. It is a slow and expensive process however, and unless exceptionally high quality is essential, a number of quicker and cheaper photocopy methods can be used.

PRINTING THE COPIES

Small offset lithographic printing is based on the same principle as ordinary offset lithographic printing, and is carried out using machines like the one shown in Figure 2.11.

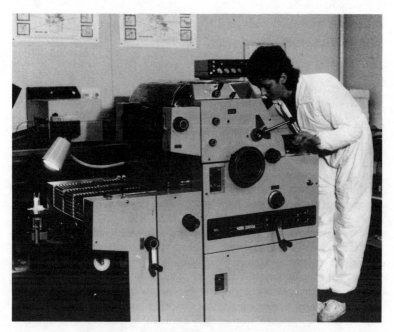

Figure 2.11 **A small offset litho printing press**

The lithographic process involves producing a master plate on which the image area is greasy (so that it repels water but attracts ink) whereas the remainder is kept clear of grease (so that it attracts water). Thus if the plate is first coated with water and then with ink, the water will adhere to the non-image areas only, preventing the ink from adhering to these areas when it is applied; the ink will thus only adhere to the image area. In the offset lithographic process, the ink that adheres to the image area of the master is first transferred to a rubber offset cylinder and hence to the copy paper, so that the paper and master never actually come in direct contact. This prevents the surface of the plate from being damaged by the hard, rough paper. The process is shown schematically in Figure 2.12.

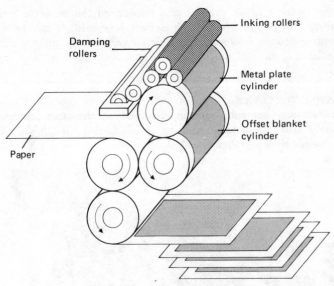

Figure 2.12 **The offset lithographic process**

Advantages of small offset litho include its great versatility (it can reproduce images of virtually all types – including photographic images), the high quality of the material produced, and its low running costs, which can make it economical for print runs as low as 30 copies in some cases. The main disadvantages of this system are its high capital cost (for all but the most basic machines) and the fact that it normally has to be run by specialist staff. Thus most organizations who install small offset litho have to centralize the service via a central reprographic unit or similar set-up. This inevitably causes delays when staff require materials since, unlike (say) a local photocopier or hectograph duplicator, the system is not directly available to them.

Choosing which Method to Use

In some cases a teacher, instructor or trainee who wants to produce multiple copies of handouts or similar materials will have very little choice as to how this can be done, being restricted to whatever reprographic system happens to be available in his institution. In other cases, a variety of systems may well be available, and then it will be necessary to decide which system is most suitable for the particular job he has in mind. Obviously, this choice will depend on a number of factors, including such things as the nature of the material to be copied, the number of copies required, the quality required, whether colour is needed, the urgency with which the material is required, cost constraints, and so on. Thus anyone who wanted to produce (say) 30 copies of a single-sheet handout for use in a lesson due to take place later in the same morning or afternoon would probably have to use either a photocopier or a hectograph duplicator, with the final choice depending on availability, personal preference and whether more than one colour was required. Someone wanting to produce 300 copies of a 50-page set of lecture notes for distribution to students at the start of the following term, on the other hand, would probably either have the material typed on stencils and have the sets run off by a technician or member of the clerical staff, or make use of the high-speed photo-copying or small offset litho facilities available in a central reprographic unit. He would not, in this case, try to do the job himself on (say) a small local photocopier, because this would not only be highly expen-sive, but would take an inordinately long time and probably burn out the machine in the process.

A summary of the respective advantages and disadvantages of the four main reprographic methods available to teachers, instructors and trainers is given in Figure 2.13 and it is hoped that this will be of help to readers faced with making such decisions.

NOTE ON COPYRIGHT RESTRICTIONS REGARDING
MULTIPLE COPYING OF DOCUMENTS

In Figure 2.13 it is, of course, assumed that the person carrying out or instigating the production of multiple copies has the legal right to do so. If you produced the original material yourself there is generally no problem, since the author of a document automatically holds copy-right in respect thereof unless this copyright is vested in or shared with some other person or body under the terms of a contractual or other agreement (eg if the author was paid to write the material for someone else). If you did *not* produce the material yourself, on the other hand, the law of copyright strictly forbids you from making multiple copies – even for educational purposes – without the prior consent of the copyright holder (normally the author or his agent, but sometimes the organization for which he works). Anyone who breaches this law, by (say) making multiple copies of a chapter of a book for use as a hand-out to students without being authorized to do so, runs the risk of facing legal action and punitive damages – as does the organization for which he works. Thus before making multiple copies of any material, you should establish whether you are legally entitled to do so. This can be done using the following algorithm.

Method	Advantages	Disadvantages
Photocopying	☐ Simple and convenient to use. ☐ Generally directly available to staff. ☐ No special master required – can copy any material. ☐ Produces high-quality copies. ☐ No restriction on print run. ☐ Collation facilities often available.	☐ Machines expensive ☐ Machines require careful handling and regular maintenance if they are not to break down or produce inferior copies. ☐ Unit costs can be relatively high. ☐ Certain colours do not reproduce on some machines.
Hectograph duplication	☐ Simple and convenient to use. ☐ Generally directly available to staff. ☐ Machines and materials relatively inexpensive. ☐ Can produce multi-colour copies.	☐ Special master required. ☐ Quality of copies comparatively poor. ☐ Limited to small print runs (not more than 200 or so). ☐ Can be messy.
Stencil duplication	☐ Can produce fairly high-quality copies. ☐ Can produce large numbers of copies – up to several thousand. ☐ Stencils can be stored for subsequent re-use. ☐ Low unit cost per copy.	☐ Special master required. ☐ Only suitable for certain types of material. ☐ Extremely messy to use. ☐ Time may be needed for copies to dry after printing.
Small offset litho	☐ Extremely versatile – can produce virtually all types of material. ☐ Can produce extremely high quality copies. ☐ Can produce large numbers of copies (tens of thousands, if necessary). ☐ Unit costs extremely low on long print runs.	☐ Special master required. ☐ Equipment expensive, and normally involves centralized operation.

Figure 2.13 **Advantages and disadvantages of different reprographic methods**

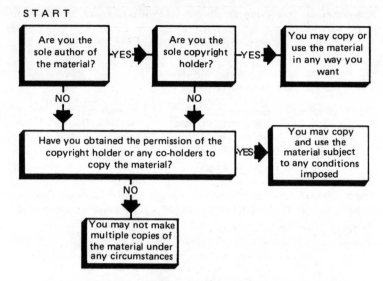

Figure 2.14 Algorithm for establishing entitlement to make multiple copies of material

Bibliography

Anderson, R H (1976) *Selecting and Developing Media for Instruction.* Van Nostrand Reinhold, Cincinnati (Chapter 8).

Beavis, R and Weatherley, C (1980) *Worksheets and School Learning.* Scottish Council for Educational Technology, Glasgow.

Ellington, H I, Addinall, E and Percival, F (1982) *A Handbook of Game Design.* Kogan Page, London/Nichols Publishing Company, New York.

Ellington, H I, Addinall, E and Percival, F (1984) *Case Studies in Game Design* Kogan Page, London/Nichols Publishing Company, New York.

Hartley, J (1985) *Designing Instructional Text* (2nd edn). Kogan Page, London/Nichols Publishing Company, New York.

Johnstone, A H and Percival, F (1981) Attention breaks in lectures. *Education in Chemistry*, **13**, 3, pp. 49-50.

Kirkland, G (1978) *Reprography: a Basic Guide.* Jordanhill College of Education, Glasgow.

Lewis, R (1981) *How To Write Self-Study Materials.* Council for Educational Technology, London.

Megarry, J (1978) *Programmed Learning: Writing a Programme.* Jordanhill College of Education, Glasgow.

New, P G (1975) *Reprography for Librarians.* Clive Bingley Ltd, London.

Rowntree, D (1966) *Basically Branching.* Macdonald.

Rowntree, D and Conners, B (eds) (1980) *How to Develop Self-Instructional Teaching. A Self-Instructional Guide to the Writing of Self-Instructional Materials.*

Published Packages from which Specimen
Material is Included in Chapter

Alternative Energy Project. Written by H I Ellington and E Addinall. Published by Association for Science Education, Hatfield (1980).
Central Heating Project. Written by H I Ellington and E Addinall. Published by Association for Science Education, Hatfield (1980).
Cheques. Published internally by the Royal Bank of Scotland, Edinburgh (1982).
The Nuclear Debate. Written by H I Ellington and E Addinall. Published by Scottish Council for Educational Technology, Glasgow (1984)
Which Material? Written by H I Ellington and E Addinall. Published by Scottish Curriculum Development Service, Dundee Centre (1984).

Chapter 3

How to Produce Non-Projected Display Materials

Introduction

In Chapter 1 we saw that the various non-documentary materials that can be displayed to or studied by learners without the need for an optical or electronic projector constitute some of the most basic — and most useful — of all teaching and learning aids. In this chapter, we will carry out a detailed examination of such materials, starting by taking a general look at how they can be used in different instructional situations. After this we will examine the main types of non-projected materials in turn, looking first at chalkboard and markerboard displays, then at 'adhesive' displays (feltboards, hook-and-loop boards and magnetic boards), then at charts, posters and other flat display materials and finally at three-dimensional display materials (mobiles, models, and so on). In each case, we will identify the main uses of the materials and show how they can be produced 'in-house' by teachers, instructors and trainers.

How Non-Projected Display Materials can be Used in Different Teaching/Learning Situations

Like printed and duplicated materials, non-projected display materials can be used in a wide range of instructional situations, covering all three of the basic classes identified in Chapter 1. Let us now examine their potential role in each.

Mass Instruction

This is probably where non-projected display materials are capable of making their most important contribution. Indeed, many of the materials that fall into the category are specifically designed for use as visual aids during expository teaching of one form or another. In such teaching their role is, of course, entirely supportive.

Individualized Instruction

Although some types of non-projected display materials are of little or no use in individualized instruction, others are capable of playing an extremely useful role. Models, for example, can be used in a wide range of self-instructional situations, as can various types of realia (eg geological and biological specimens). In most cases, such materials play a key role in the instruction process by providing the actual objects of study.

Group Learning

Many non-projected display materials can also play a useful supportive role in group-learning situations, eg by providing visual aids during presentation/discussion-type activities such as seminars and tutorials or providing the subject matter for small-group exercises.

All these various uses of non-projected display materials will be discussed in greater detail in the sections that deal with specific types of materials.

Chalkboard and Markerboard Displays

The first group of non-projected display media that we will consider are the various dark-coloured surfaces on which displays can be written or drawn using chalk (chalkboards) and the various light-coloured surfaces on which similar displays can be produced using suitable markers, pens or crayons (markerboards). Let us now look at these in turn.

Chalkboards

The chalkboard (or blackboard as it was called until it was realized that such boards were very seldom black any longer) is so much a part of classrooms that it has become a symbol for education itself. Indeed, until the development of the overhead projector during the 1940s and its more recent spread into virtually every classroom and lecture theatre, the chalkboard was probably the most important of all instructional aids (apart from the printed page). Even today such boards are still a standard fixture in virtually all teaching and training environments, although their use is by no means as automatic and universal as was the case in the past.

THE DIFFERENT TYPES OF CHALKBOARD
When I started school practically all chalkboards were still black, consisting of large sheets of wood covered with matt black paint. Since then most such boards have been replaced by other types of surface, such as cloth, various forms of plastic and other synthetic materials. In addition most chalkboards are now coloured, the most common colour being green and other widely used colours being blue and brown. This is because coloured boards have been found to produce less glare and reflection, are less prone to 'ghosting' (marks left when the chalk is rubbed out), and, in general, provide greater legibility than the traditional 'blackboard'.

Another comparatively recent development in the evolution of the chalkboard has been the appearance of the magnetic chalkboard — a surface made of ferro-magnetic material covered with a thin layer of dark-coloured vitreous particles. This can be used in the same ways as magnetic markerboards, and will be discussed later in the chapter.

HOW CHALKBOARDS SHOULD (AND SHOULD NOT) BE USED

Traditionally, the chalkboard was used in virtually every situation where textual, mathematical or graphical material had to be displayed to a class or small group — and, in some establishments, is still so used. Certainly it is a versatile, inexpensive and useful teaching aid and, if a teacher, instructor or trainer so wishes, can be used for such straightforward expository purposes as:

☐ The systematic display of virtually the entire subject matter of a lecture or taught lesson to a class.
☐ The display of a 'skeleton guide' to such a lecture or lesson, eg in the form of a set of section and sub-section headings.
☐ The display of specific items (maps, diagrams, tables, etc) during such a lecture or lesson.

I would, however, seriously suggest that all these functions can be fulfilled just as effectively — and a great deal more conveniently — by use of the overhead projector. What, for example, is the point of laboriously copying a lengthy mathematical proof, scientific derivation or complicated map or diagram on to a chalkboard, only to have to rub it out after it has been used once? Would it not be much more sensible to produce a permanent copy of the material in overhead transparency form, so that it can be used again and again?

It is now generally acknowledged that the most appropriate — and most effective — way of using the chalkboard in the modern classroom is as a means of displaying impromptu material (words, equations, diagrams, etc that have become necessary due to an unexpected turn in a lesson) and material which is developed in the course of the lesson by interaction with the class (ideas produced by buzz groups, experimental results, solutions to tutorial exercises, and so on). Thus, it is still strongly advisable that teachers, instructors and trainers should take the trouble to become reasonably proficient in the use of the chalkboard so that they can cope effectively with such 'off-the-cuff' requirements.

HOW TO DEVELOP BASIC CHALKBOARD SKILLS

Despite its long tradition of use, many teachers and trainers find the chalkboard a difficult medium to handle — often simply because they have never taken the trouble to master the necessary basic techniques. Many people, for example, hold the chalk the wrong way — holding it like a pen or pencil rather than in the correct way shown in Figure 3.1 overleaf. As can be seen, the chalk should be held between the fingers and thumb, with the non-writing end pointing in towards the palm of the hand, and should be presented to the board at a fairly low angle.

Also, many people make the mistake of trying to use the fingers to write with the chalk, as they would with a pen or pencil. The correct technique is to use the fingers and thumb simply as a chuck to hold the chalk, and to use the entire hand to make the writing stroke, executing the stroke by movements of the shoulder joint and (to a lesser extent) by wrist, elbow and body movements. Some other useful points of technique are given below.

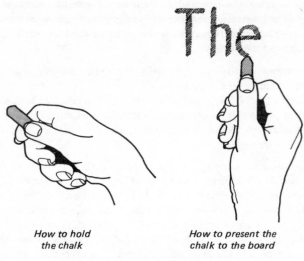

How to hold
the chalk

How to present the
chalk to the board

Figure 3.1

☐ Rotate the chalk slightly as you make each stroke, and change to a new facet of the chalk face for each new stroke or word (this helps to keep the lines of uniform thickness).

☐ Always try to place the chalk length in line with the stroke being drawn, so that the chalk is pulled across the board (note that this may necessitate the wrist being placed in an awkward position).

☐ Stand in such a position that you can reach the board easily with the elbow of your writing arm only slightly bent.

☐ Use body sway and bending of the knees to reach different parts of the board during a stroke, keeping a balanced stance throughout.

☐ Try to develop a clear writing or printing style that can be read without difficulty from the back of the classroom in which you are working; check this by going to the back of the room yourself.

☐ Leave generous spaces between words — this greatly increases legibility.

☐ Always try to achieve a neat, systematic lay-out, with level, uniformly spaced lines of writing; if necessary, draw light guidelines on the board using a chalkboard ruler or T-square.

The subject of basic chalkboard technique is dealt with in much greater length in the book by Pringle that is listed in the Bibliography, and interested readers are referred to this. The book by Mugglestone also provides useful information on how to use the chalkboard effectively.

SOME USEFUL METHODS OF PRODUCING GRAPHIC DISPLAYS

For the benefit of those who still like to use the chalkboard to display graphic material such as maps and diagrams, let us now examine some of the 'tricks of the trade' that can be used to produce such displays. Some people, of course, have no need to resort to such methods, since they possess the artistic and graphic skills to produce all such material freehand.

The grid method: This is one of the simplest methods of producing an enlarged version of graphic material, whether on a chalkboard, marker-board, or any other medium. It involves covering the material to be copied with a pattern of square grid lines, either by drawing the lines on the material itself or by covering it with a transparent sheet on which the grid has been drawn. (I recommend the latter method since the grid, once prepared, is available for future use.) If a similar grid, scaled up by whatever factor is required, is now lightly drawn on to the surface on which the enlarged copy is to be made (or, even better, projected on to the surface using an opaque or overhead projector), the resulting grid lines will probably enable even the least talented of artists to produce a reasonable copy of the original material.

The projection method: This is another standard technique that can be used to produce enlarged versions of graphic or photographic materials on surfaces of all types. It involves projecting a suitably enlarged image of the original material on to the surface and then tracing over the outline and whatever other detail one wishes to reproduce. Note that the method can be used with both transparent and opaque originals by using the appropriate type of projector — a slide projector for photographic slides, a filmstrip projector for filmstrip frames, an overhead projector for large transparencies and an art aid or opaque projector for photographic prints and other opaque items. Also note that an ordinary overhead projector can be used as a makeshift opaque projector by placing the material to be copied on the platen, image side upwards, and illuminating the material from above using a portable lamp of some sort (see Figure 3.3).

The template method: Another technique that can be used to draw outline figures on both chalkboards and marker boards is the template method. This is particularly useful in cases where standard shapes (eg maps, scientific apparatus, geometrical figures or dress patterns) have to be drawn repeatedly with some accuracy. It involves preparing a suitable template of the shape using some suitable stiff, lightweight material such as thin sheet metal, thick card, plywood or rigid plastic, a template that can then be placed on the board and traced round whenever the shape has to be drawn. Templates can be produced from smaller originals by drawing them on a sheet of the chosen material using the projection method described above. It is, incidentally, a good idea to fit such templates with a handle of some sort to make it easier to hold them against the board while in use.

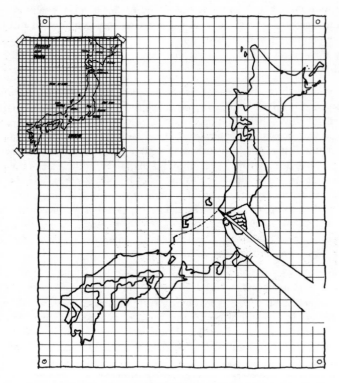

Figure 3.2 **The grid method of producing enlarged copies of graphic material**

The pounce pattern method: This is another method that can be used to reproduce standard shapes which have to be drawn repeatedly and with accuracy. It involves first producing a line drawing of the required shape on a large sheet of paper or thin card, and then punching small holes along the lines at regular intervals (between ¼ inch and 1 inch apart, depending on the detail required). With paper, this can be done using a special tool fitted with a spiked wheel, which is run along the lines when the paper is placed on a suitable surface (eg a sheet of soft wood). With card, the holes can be punched out using a leather worker's punch or similar device. If the completed pounce pattern is now placed flat against the surface of the chalkboard, held in position using strips of adhesive tape, and the lines to be drawn lightly tapped with the face of a dusty chalkboard eraser, the outline of the shape will be transferred on to the board in the form of lines of dots. These can then be joined up to produce the required figure. By preparing such pounce patterns before lessons, it is possible to impress classes considerably by the ease and skill with which you apparently draw complicated diagrams freehand.

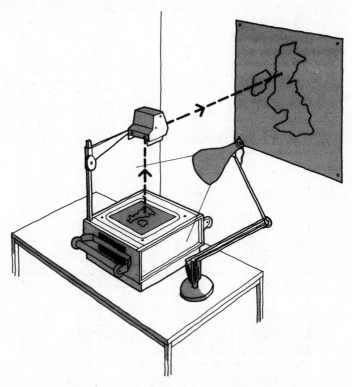

Figure 3.3 **Using an overhead projector and desk lamp to produce an enlarged projection of an image on an opaque medium**

The above techniques are described in more detail in the books by Wittich and Schuller and by Minor and Frye listed in the Bibliography.

Markerboards

These boards, which are also known as whiteboards, are sometimes fitted in teaching rooms instead of conventional chalkboards. They consist of large sheets of white or light-coloured plastic material with a surface texture suitable for writing or drawing on using felt pens, markers or crayons, and can be used in much the same way as chalkboards. They have, however, a number of advantages over the latter.

There is, first of all, none of the mess that always results when chalk — even the 'dustless' variety — is used. Second, a much wider range of colours and tone strengths can be used, and the resulting display is invariably sharper, better defined and clearer than is possible using chalk. Third, a markerboard — unlike a chalkboard — can double up as a projection screen if required.

There is, however, one possible problem that can arise with marker-boards: difficulty in cleaning the surface properly so that 'ghost' marks are not left behind. For this reason, it is strongly advisable to use only the types of marker pens or crayons that are recommended by the manufacturer of the particular board you are using, and to make sure that you know how the board should be cleaned. In some cases this can be done simply by wiping with a dry or damp cloth, while in others a special cleaning fluid or solvent is required. If this is the case, always make sure that a supply is readily available — together with a suitable cloth or eraser.

The techniques for producing displays on markerboards are basically the same as those just described for chalkboards.

Adhesive Displays

The second major class of non-projected display materials that we will look at are those where the display is stuck to the display surface in some way (other than by drawing pins or glue). The most important members of the class are feltboard displays, hook-and-loop board displays and magnetic board displays, which will now be examined in turn.

Feltboard Displays

The feltboard (which is also known as the flannel-board or flannel-graph) relies on the fact that shapes cut out of felt, flannel or similar fabrics will adhere to display surfaces covered with like material. Such systems can be used both to create permanent or semi-permanent wall-mounted displays, but their most important application is in situations requiring the movement or rearrangement of pieces. They are, for example, ideal for displaying things like table settings, demonstrating changes in plant layouts or corporate structures, showing how words can be joined together to form phrases and sentences, and illustrating basic arithmetical and geometrical concepts. One such application (demonstration that the area of a triangle is equal to half the product of the length of its base and its height) is shown opposite. As can be seen, it simply involves displaying a felt triangle that is composed of three pieces (Figure 3.4(a)) and then moving the two smaller pieces to the positions shown in Figure 3.4(b).

MAKING YOUR OWN FELTBOARD
Although ready-made feltboards can be bought from educational

suppliers, it is a very simple matter to make your own. All you need is a large sheet of felt or flannel, which can either be pinned to a convenient wall or bulletin board or stuck to a suitably sized sheet of plywood or hardboard, thus producing a portable display surface that can be set up on an easel wherever it is required.

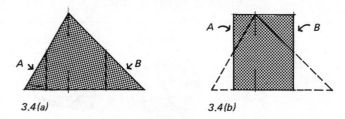

Figure 3.4 Use of a feltboard to show that the area of a triangle
= ½ base x height

PRODUCING FELTBOARD DISPLAY MATERIALS
Feltboard materials, designed for use in a wide range of instructional situations, are available commercially but it is again a very simple matter to create your own. The required shapes (like the ones shown in Figure 3.3) can simply be cut from any convenient sheet of felt or flannel (of a different colour from the display surface) and can be made even more cheaply from felt-embossed wallpaper. If you are planning to make regular use of home-produced feltboard displays, purchase of a roll of this wallpaper will provide you with an almost unlimited supply of the necessary raw materials at very low cost — especially if you can get hold of an 'end-of-line' bargain roll. Use of embossed wallpaper for the preparation of feltboard display materials has the added advantage of providing a light surface on which words or letters can be written, images drawn, etc. If you want to produce more rigid display materials, these can be cut from thin card and then backed with felt or embossed wallpaper in order to make them stick to the feltboard.

Hook-And-Loop Board Displays

The hook-and-loop board (which is also known as a teazle board or teazle graph) works on the same basic principle as the feltboard. In this case, however, the display materials are backed with special fabric (such as velcro) which incorporates large numbers of tiny hooks, while the display surface is covered with material incorporating tiny loops with which the hooks can engage. This creates a much stronger bond than that which is formed between two pieces of felt, thus allowing much heavier display materials to be attached to the surface of a hook-and-loop board. Such boards can be used for much the same purposes as feltboards, but only offer a real advantage over the latter in situations where the material being displayed is heavy — demonstrating the components of an actual piece of equipment, for example, or displaying items of realia as shown in Figure 3.5.

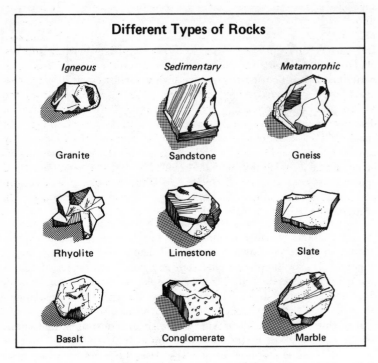

Different Types of Rocks

| Igneous | Sedimentary | Metamorphic |

Granite   Sandstone   Gneiss

Rhyolite   Limestone   Slate

Basalt   Conglomerate   Marble

Figure 3.5 **Use of a hook-and-loop board to display rock samples which have had strips of hook tape cemented to flat surfaces filed or ground on their backs**

MAKING YOUR OWN DISPLAY BOARD
Hook-and-loop display boards can be made in exactly the same way as feltboards, ie by getting hold of a suitable piece of fabric (available from educational supply companies) and either pinning this to a convenient wall or bulletin board or producing a portable board by sticking or pinning it to a piece of plywood or hardboard.

PRODUCING DISPLAY MATERIALS
Objects of virtually any type can be prepared for use in hook-and-loop displays by attaching suitable strips or pads of hook tape to their backs. Such tapes are available in a number of forms, including dry adhesive-backed, pressure sensitive adhesive-backed, solvent activated adhesive-backed, and non adhesive-backed.

Magnetic Boards

Even more useful and versatile than feltboards and hook-and-loop boards are the various forms of magnetic board. These come in two main forms — the magnetic chalkboards that were described on page 71 and magnetic markerboards (sheets of ferro-magnetic material with specially painted light surfaces on which material can be written or drawn using suitable markers or pens). Both types of board enable display items made of or backed with magnetic material to be stuck to and moved about on their surfaces, and both enable this moveable display to be supplemented by writing or drawing on the board. Thus, magnetic boards can be used to produce highly sophisticated displays that enable movement and change in systems to be clearly demonstrated to a class or small group. They are, for example, the ideal medium for demonstrating military tactics or carrying out sports coaching. For coaching a basketball or football team, for example, the field of play can be painted permanently on the board, with the individual players being identified by clearly marked magnetic discs that can be rearranged and moved about as and when required and the various movements, run patterns, etc being shown by adding suitable arrows or lines using chalk or marker pen.

Figure 3.6 **Use of a magnetic board in sports coaching**

MAKING YOUR OWN MAGNETIC BOARD
Both magnetic chalkboards and magnetic markerboards can be made using readily available materials and, although such boards will probably

not prove as satisfactory as commercially purchased versions, they can be used to fulfil exactly the same basic functions. In both cases the basic board should be made from a thin sheet of ferro-magnetic material such as mild steel, which should preferably be mounted on a thicker sheet of wood or chipboard in order to give it the required rigidity. To produce a magnetic chalkboard, the surface should be painted with a suitable dark-coloured matt paint, while to produce a magnetic marker board, a suitable light-coloured silk or gloss paint should be used.

PRODUCING MAGNETIC DISPLAY MATERIALS
There are two main ways of producing such materials. The first is to make them out of special magnetic rubber, which is available in sheet and strip form. The second is to make them out of non-magnetic material such as stiff card and then to stick strips of magnetic rubber or small magnets to their backs, so that they will adhere to the board. A wide range of ready-made materials such as magnetic letters and numbers that can be used to form displays is also available from educational suppliers.

Charts, Posters and Similar Flat Display Materials

The various forms of chart, poster and other flat pictorial display materials have always been among the most useful and versatile visual aids at the disposal of teachers and instructors of all types. Let us now look in turn at some of the more important varieties.

Flipcharts

These constitute a simple and, when used in an appropriate context, highly effective method of displaying information to a class or small group. Such charts consist of a number of large sheets of paper, fixed to a support bar, easel or display board by clamping or pinning them along their top edges so that they can be flipped backwards or forwards as required.

Such charts can be used in two basic ways. First, they can be used to display a succession of pre-prepared sheets, which can be shown in the required order either by flipping them into view from the back of the suspension system one by one or by revealing each successive sheet by flipping the previous one over the back of the suspension system out of the way. If the former method is to be used, the sheets should be clamped to the display system in reverse order of showing, ie with the one to be shown last uppermost; with the latter method, the sheets should be clamped to the display system in the correct order of showing, ie with the one to be shown first uppermost. When preparing such flipchart sequences, it is best to keep the message or information on each sheet fairly simple, since this increases their impact. Also it is obviously essential to make sure that they can be read or seen clearly by all the members of the class or group; again you should check this by inspecting them from the back of the class or the furthest distance from which they have to be viewed.

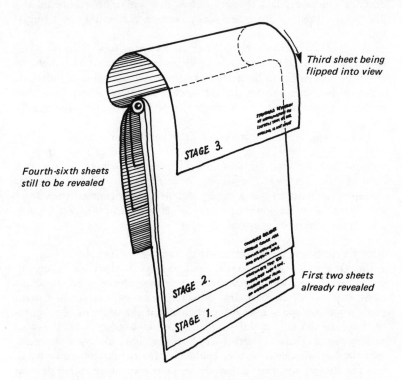

Figure 3.7 **Use of a set of pre-prepared flipcharts to show the various stages of a six-stage process by progressively building up the complete process**

The other main way in which flipcharts can be used is by providing an instantly renewable series of blank surfaces on which material can be jotted down on an impromptu basis in the course of a lesson, group discussion or other activity. They can, for example, be used to list replies from class members to questions or ideas generated by buzz groups.

Charts and Wallcharts

The various forms of chart and wallchart have always been popular in all sectors of education and training because of their versatility and ease of use and, even with the spread of more sophisticated visual aids such as slides, films and videos, are still capable of playing an important role in such work. Although the distinction between charts and wallcharts is sometimes a bit blurred, the former term is generally taken to refer to displays on large sheets of paper or cloth that are designed to be shown to a class or group in the course of a lesson. The latter term is used to describe similar displays that are pinned to a wall or bulletin board and are mainly intended for casual study outwith the context of a formal lesson.

Another distinction between the two groups is that the material on charts is usually larger and easier to see or read than that on wallcharts, since the former has to be clearly distinguishable or legible at a distance whereas the latter can be studied at close quarters. Apart from this, however, the principles that underlie the design of the two are basically the same.

One of the great advantages of both charts and wallcharts is that they can be made fairly large, and can thus contain far more complicated and more detailed displays than it would be possible to incorporate on (say) an overhead transparency or a 35 mm slide. They can, for example, be used to show highly detailed maps (one of their most important and most universal uses) and detailed structural, taxonomic, and organizational diagrams of all types.

HOW TO PRODUCE YOUR OWN CHARTS AND WALLCHARTS

Although a wide range of charts and wallcharts is available commercially or as good-will 'giveaways' from industrial and other organizations, it is still often necessary to make one's own in order to cover a given topic in a specific way — particularly if the topic to be taught is of a specialized or unusual nature. Before embarking on the task of making up a chart or wallchart, however, it is always worthwhile investigating whether one that could be used for the job you have in mind is already available, either within your own organization or from an external source (from a central resources centre, an educational supplier, an industrial or other organization, and so on); if it is, you could save yourself a great deal of time and effort.

If you do decide to go ahead with the production of your chart, you should bear the following basic principles in mind:

☐ Make the chart and all items on it big enough to be seen clearly by the entire class or group that you will be using it with or, in the case of a wallchart, in the context within which it is to be used.

☐ Aim for maximum clarity, using a layout and printing technique that make the 'message' that you are trying to get across perfectly clear.

☐ Do not make the chart unnecessarily complicated, especially with a chart designed for display to a class during a lesson; too much detail may well lead to loss of clarity and/or confusion.

☐ Try to make the chart visually attractive, using colour if at all possible.

Some useful standard formats that can be used as the basis of charts are shown opposite.

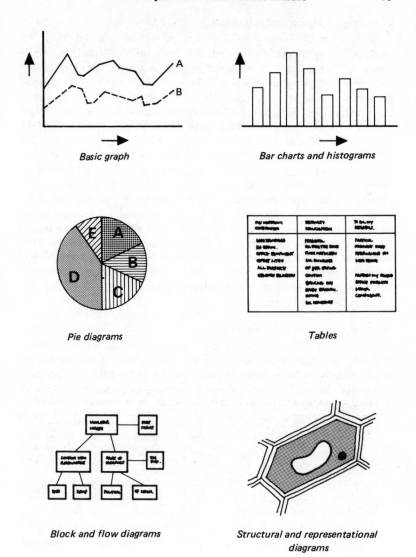

Basic graph

Bar charts and histograms

Pie diagrams

Tables

Block and flow diagrams

Structural and representational diagrams

Figure 3.8 Some standard formats that can be used in charts

PRODUCING THE GRAPHIC MATERIAL

In many cases, the main graphic content of a chart or wallchart can be produced using simple drawing aids such as a ruler, T-square and compasses. In some cases, however, it may be necessary to reproduce a complicated drawing or schematic diagram, often from a smaller original contained in a book or magazine. In such cases, two of the techniques suggested earlier for producing similar drawings on chalkboards and markerboards — the grid method (page 73) and the projection method (page 73) should prove useful.

If the original drawing is larger than the version that you want to produce, however, a variation of the projection method known as reverse projection may be employed. This makes use of the fact that all optical systems are reversible, so that a system such as the lens of an overhead projector, which is normally used to throw an enlarged image of the material on its platen on to a screen, can also be used to produce a reduced image of a poster, chart, etc on the surface of the platen. This technique, which may have to be carried out in a partially darkened room, involves illuminating the material to be copied with floodlights and copying the resulting reduced image behind a suitable shield. The set-up is shown in Figure 3.9.

PRODUCING LETTERING ON CHARTS

If you possess the necessary graphic skills, it is possible to produce perfectly clear and acceptable lettering on charts by freehand use of appropriate pens or markers. Most people find this difficult, however, and prefer to use one of the many lettering aids that are available. These include the following:

☐ *Instant lettering*, in the form of dry transfer letters on plastic sheets that can be transferred to the work by rubbing with a burnisher, rounded pencil point or. ball point pen. This produces high-quality results if used properly, but is expensive.

☐ *Stencils*, usually in the form of transparent plastic strips carrying the complete alphabet in a given style and size. These can produce reasonably good results, but not of the quality of transfer lettering or some of the other methods described below.

☐ *Template lettering guides*; such systems (of which the best known is manufactured by Leroy) make use of a special pen fitted with a tracing pin that is moved round the shapes of the letters in the guide. They can produce better results than stencils, and are also quicker; they are, however, more expensive.

☐ *Lettering machines*, which operate on the 'Dymo' principle and can be used to print lines of lettering on special adhesive ribbon; the ribbon can then be cut into sections, and laid out in the required way. These can also produce very good results, but are again comparatively expensive to use.

☐ *Phototypesetting*: use of a word processor-like device to compose text, which is produced in the form of a photographic negative that can be used to produce a positive print of whatever size is required. This again gives excellent results, but the equipment is expensive.

Further information about these various techniques can be found in *Techniques for Producing Visual Instructional Media* (see Bibliography).

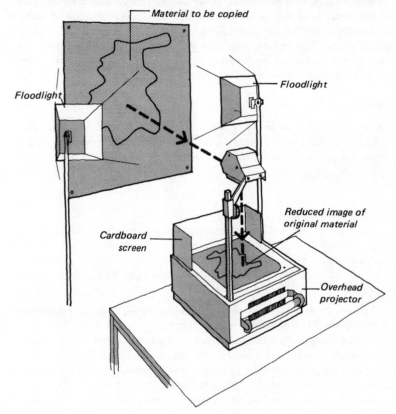

Figure 3.9 **The reverse projection technique for producing reduced images of graphic material**

ADDING COLOUR TO CHARTS
This can be done by a wide range of methods, some of the most useful of which are outlined below.

☐ Poster paint, applied with a brush: the standard method of producing bold colours on a poster or chart.
☐ Water colour paint: useful for more subtle colours, or for producing subdued washes of colour.
☐ Coloured adhesive paper: this is available in a wide range of colours; if cut to the shape required, it can produce a sharpness and finish that is difficult to achieve using paint; it is also relatively cheap.

☐ Coloured transfer films: these can be used in the same way as adhesive paper, but are much more expensive.

USING READY-MADE MATERIAL AND PHOTOGRAPHIC PRINTS

In many cases, it is possible to make use of ready-made material such as photographs or diagrams from magazines in the preparation of charts and wallcharts. This can not only save a great deal of time, but can also produce excellent results. Specially prepared photographic prints can also prove useful on occasions, especially on wallcharts and other permanent or semi-permanent displays.

Posters

These are similar in many ways to charts, but are usually smaller, simpler and bolder in content and style. Their main uses in the class-room are as a means of providing decoration, atmosphere and motiva-tion, although they can also be used to make or remind learners of key points.

PRODUCING YOUR OWN POSTERS

As with charts and wallcharts, ready-made posters are available from a large number of sources — very often free of charge. Nevertheless there are occasions when it is necessary to produce 'home-made' posters for specific purposes. When doing so, you should bear the following points in mind.

☐ To attract attention a poster should be dramatic, with any prominent or central feature(s) standing out sharply.
☐ Having caught the viewer's attention, the poster should get across its message clearly and quickly; this message should therefore be a simple one, capable of being taken in at a glance.
☐ A poster should also be visually attractive, even though its subject matter may be anything but pleasant (warnings about health hazards, the dangers of war, etc).

Apart from these points, the techniques for producing posters are basically the same as those described above for producing charts and wallcharts.

Three-Dimensional Display Materials

The final group of non-projected display materials that we will look at differ from those described so far in that they are all three-dimensional. The group includes four basic types of materials — mobiles, models, dioramas and realia — which will now be described in turn.

Mobiles

A mobile is, in essence, a three-dimensional wallchart in which the individual components can move about. Instead of displaying a related system of pictures, words, etc on the flat surface of a wall, they are drawn on card, cut out and hung independently from the roof or a suitable beam using fine threads. The resulting display, which turns and changes shape as it is affected by random air currents, acquires a vitality which can never be produced in a flat display of the same material. A typical mobile, displaying the useful products that are obtained from farm animals, is shown in Figure 3.10.

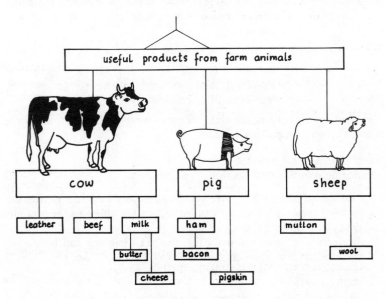

Figure 3.10 **A typical mobile, showing the products from farm animals**

Such mobiles can be suspended in a corner of a classroom, where they will not get in people's way, but will still be clearly visible to the pupils. They are particularly suitable for use with younger pupils, who are generally fascinated by the continuous movements that take place in such displays, which helps to fix the information that the mobiles carry in the children's minds.

Mobiles can be used in virtually any situation where pupils have to acquire and consolidate a set of related facts, and where a wallchart would normally be used to reinforce this material. Some specific subjects where they might prove useful include:

Basic vocabulary: Here, words can be grouped by sound, meaning, structure, etc, and mobiles constructed to illustrate whichever set of relationships is to be demonstrated. Word cards are, in fact, the simplest type of components from which mobiles can be created.

Geography: A country's exports can be arranged in related groups (minerals, agricultural products, industrial products, etc).

Biology: Related species, parts of the body, etc can be arranged in groups.

Chemistry: Related groups of elements and compounds can be displayed.

Physics: Symbols representing different forms of energy, related classes of materials, etc can be arranged in patterns.

Home economics: Related groups of foods can be displayed.

History: Related sequences of events can be represented pictorially and arranged in the correct pattern, together with their dates.

No doubt most readers can think of many more applications, including some in their own particular fields.

HOW TO CREATE A MOBILE

Producing a mobile involves three basic stages:

1. *Conceptual design* This involves choosing the basic theme for the mobile, deciding what items to include and establishing the patterns that you want to illustrate.
2. *Production of components* This involves designing and producing the individual components, which may be simple word cards, cut-out models, symbols or even items of realia (which can make effective mobiles).
3. *Assembly and mounting* This is the most difficult part, and is best done by first assembling the simplest groups of items, then combinations of such groups, and so on until a balanced, freely moving display is achieved. At each stage, the correct position for suspension should be determined by trial and error. The final display should be hung from a hook or drawing pin *firmly* fixed into the ceiling, or from a wooden rod fixed across a corner of the room at a suitable height (such a rod can be used as a permanent suspension system for mobiles).

Models

Models (ie recognizable three-dimensional representations of real things or abstract systems) can play a useful role in a wide range of instructional situations. They are, however, particularly useful in three specific roles, namely as visual support materials in mass instruction, as objects for study or manipulation in individualized learning, and as construction projects for individuals, small groups or even entire classes. When using models in the first of these roles, however, it should be remembered that even the best three-dimensional model invariably appears two-dimensional except to those who are very close, so it is usually worth-while getting the learners to gather round the model when its salient features are being demonstrated; unless you do this, you could prob-ably achieve the same objectives in most cases by using a two-dimensional representation such as a slide or OHP transparency.

Some specific applications of models are listed below:

☐ They can be used to reduce very large objects and enlarge very small objects to a size that can be conveniently observed and handled.

☐ They can be used to demonstrate the interior structures of objects or systems with a clarity that is often not possible with two-dimensional representations (eg the crystal models shown in Figure 3.11).

☐ They can be used to demonstrate movement — another feature that it is often difficult to show adequately using two-dimensional dis-play systems.

☐ They can be used to represent a highly complex situation or process in a simplified way that can easily be understood by learners. This can be done by concentrating only on essential features, eliminating all the complex and often confusing details that are so often present in real-life systems.

MAKING YOUR OWN MODELS
The range of methods available for making models for instructional purposes is enormous, but readers may find some of the following standard techniques useful.

☐ Use of commercially available kits of parts, such as the ball-and-spring systems that are used to make models of molecules and the various types of tube-and-spigot systems that can be used to make models of crystals (as shown in Figure 3.11).

☐ Use of construction systems such as Meccano and Fisher-Price to make working models.

☐ Use of inexpensive materials such as cardboard, hardboard, wood and wire to make up static models of all types (models of buildings, geometrical bodies and three-dimensional shapes, and so on).

☐ Use of materials like modelling clay and plasticine to produce realis-tic models of animals, anatomical demonstrations, and so on.

☐ Use of materials like plaster of Paris and papier mâché to produce model landscapes.

Dioramas

These are still display systems that combine a three-dimensional fore-ground of model buildings, figures, etc with a two-dimensional painted background, thus creating a highly realistic effect. They can be used in the teaching of a wide range of subjects, including:

☐ History, drama, religious studies (representations of historical or dramatic scenes, battles, etc).

☐ Geography and geology (representations of towns, landscapes, pre-historic landscapes and scenes, etc).

☐ Biology and natural history (representations of animals in their natural habitats).

Figure 3.11 **Models of crystals made up from 'do-it-yourself' kits of parts**

PRODUCING A DIORAMA

Although sophisticated dioramas of the type that are seen in museums can be expensive, time-consuming and difficult to make up, it is perfectly possible for anyone possessing even the most basic of graphic and artistic skills to produce highly effective displays of this type.

This can be done as follows.

1. Make a semi-circular base of the required size out of chipboard, hardboard, thick card or some other suitable material.

2. Make up a strip of thin white card of suitable height that is capable of extending all the way round the curved side of the base, draw and/or paint the required background scene on this, and fix it to the base (eg with drawing pins).

3. Build up any landscape required in the foreground using plaster of Paris or papier mâché, and paint this in the required colour(s).

4. Produce or acquire any materials that are required for the foreground and set them in position; such materials can include model figures

(cardboard cut-outs, plasticine models, etc), model buildings, model trees, model ships, tanks or other vehicles, pieces of rock, and any other materials that you feel will enhance the realism of the scene being depicted.

The basic features of a typical diorama representing a religious scene are shown in Figure 3.12.

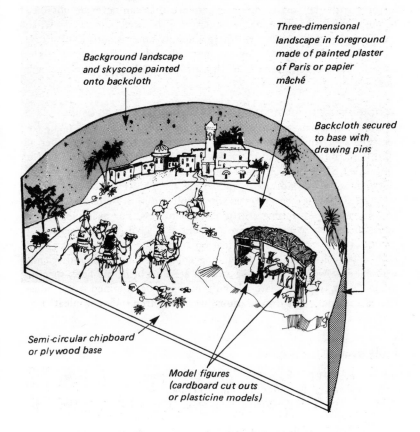

Three-dimensional landscape in foreground made of painted plaster of Paris or papier mâché

Background landscape and skyscope painted onto backcloth

Backcloth secured to base with drawing pins

Semi-circular chipboard or plywood base

Model figures (cardboard cut outs or plasticine models)

Figure 3.12 **A typical diorama depicting a religious scene**

Like the construction of models, construction of dioramas can provide excellent practical projects for individuals, small groups or even whole classes.

Realia

The supreme instructional 'model' is, in some cases, the article itself, since there are often considerable advantages to be gained from letting learners see or handle the 'real thing' as opposed to a mere representation thereof. In many cases, of course, this will not be practicable on grounds of availability, accessibility, safety, expense, and so on, but there are many other cases where no such objections apply and, in such cases, serious consideration should be given to the use of realia. Such materials can be used both to support expository teaching and in individualized and group-learning situations, where they can provide learners with the sort of direct experience that can never be obtained through mediated learning, no matter how well contrived. When studying geology, for example, there is simply no satisfactory substitute for actually handling and examining real rock specimens, while the same is true of many aspects of the study of biology, physiology, and similar subjects.

ACQUIRING ITEMS OF REALIA FOR INSTRUCTIONAL PURPOSES
The way in which one sets about getting hold of items of realia for teaching or training purposes will, of course, depend on a number of factors including the nature of the item(s) required, the existence (or otherwise) of convenient local sources of supply, the financial resources one has at one's disposal, and so on. It is, however, often possible to acquire specific items or even whole collections of items at very little cost merely by exercising a little resourcefulness. For example, I once built up a fairly comprehensive collection of geological specimens at practically no cost by a combination of visiting local sources armed with a large hammer and persuading colleagues, relatives and friends who I knew would be visiting certain areas to bring me back specific items. Other types of material can sometimes be obtained from industrial firms and other organisations, who are often only too pleased to help.

Bibliography

Anderson, R H (1976) *Selecting and Developing Media for Instruction*. Van Nostrand Reinhold, Cincinnati (Chapter 9).

Cable R (1965) *Audio-Visual Handbook*. University of London Press (Chapter 1).

Dale, E (1969) *Audiovisual Methods in Teaching*. Holt, Rinehart and Winston, New York.

Kemp, J E (1980) *Planning and Producing Audiovisual Materials*. Harper and Row, Publishers Inc, New York.

Minor, E and Frye, H R (1970) *Techniques for Producing Visual Instructional Media*. McGraw Hill, New York.

Mugglestone, P (1980) *Planning and Using the Blackboard*. George Allen & Unwin Ltd, London.

Pringle, B (1966) *Chalk Illustration*. Pergamon Press, Oxford.

Romiszowski, A J (1974) *The Selection and Use of Instructional Media.* Kogan Page, London (Chapter 4).

Wittich, W A and Schuller, C F (1979) *Instructional Technology — Its Nature and Use.* Harper and Row, New York.

Chapter 4

How to Produce Still Projected Display Materials

Introduction

In this chapter, we will turn our attention to the third major group of still display materials: those that require some sort of optical projector or viewer to enable them to be shown to or studied by learners. This category includes two of the most important and most widely used of all visual aids: overhead projector transparencies and slides, both of which will be examined in detail.

As usual, we will begin the chapter by taking a general look at how still projected display materials can be used in the three main classes of instructional situations that were identified in Chapter 1. Next, we will look in turn at the two types of still projected materials mentioned above — OHP transparencies and photographic slides. In each case, we will again identify the main uses of the materials and offer guidance on how they may be produced.

How Still Projected Display Materials can be Used in Different Teaching/Learning Situations

Like the other two classes of still display materials, still projected materials can be used in virtually all types of teaching/learning situation, covering all three of the areas identified in Chapter 1 (mass instruction, individualized instruction and group learning). Let us now look briefly at the role that they are capable of playing in each.

Mass Instruction

This is where still projected materials are capable of making their greatest contribution to the instructional process and is, in fact, the area for which most such materials were specifically developed. Indeed, it is probably true to say that one of the media involved — the overhead projector — is the most useful single display aid available to anyone who wishes to carry out expository instruction of virtually any type. The role of still projected materials in such instruction is, of course, entirely supportive.

Individualized Instruction

Still projected materials — particularly slides and filmstrips — are also capable of playing a key role in individualized instruction, particularly when used in conjunction with audio materials. This role will be examined in greater detail in Chapter 6.

Group Learning

Many still projected display materials are also capable of playing a useful supportive role in many group-learning situations. The overhead projector, for example, is the ideal vehicle for learners to use to present visual material at seminars, group discussions, etc and also during group exercises such as games and simulations. Slides and filmstrips can also be used to provide illustrative material in such exercises.

Overhead Projector Transparencies and Similar Materials

As has already been stated, the overhead projector (OHP) is probably the most versatile and useful visual aid that can be used to support mass-instruction methods. It has already largely replaced the chalkboard as the main teaching aid in many schools, colleges and training establishments, relegating the latter to a secondary role more suited to its characteristics (the display of impromptu material, etc).

The overhead projector has a number of definite advantages over other methods of presenting visual information. A teacher or trainer can, for example, use it in exactly the same way as a chalkboard or markerboard (for writing out notes, working through calculations and proofs, drawing graphic material, and so on) but with the great advantage of always facing the class, and thus being able to maintain eye contact with the learners. Such eye contact, which is, of course, impossible when a teacher or instructor is writing on a chalkboard or markerboard, can play a useful role in expository teaching, serving both as an outward non-verbal communication channel for the teacher and as a means of obtaining feedback from a class on how a lesson is going. Another important advantage over the chalkboard or markerboard is that the OHP can also be used to show pre-prepared material, thus enabling teachers and trainers to build up banks of notes, diagrams, tables, etc that can be used over and over again. In this way teachers can gradually build up a systematic collection of 'instant lectures', covering virtually all the areas that they are called upon to teach. When well planned and designed, such sets of overhead transparencies can also provide all the cues and *aides-mémoire* that are needed during a lesson, so that no conventional teaching notes are required. Other advantages of the overhead projector are that it is clean, quiet, and 'user friendly', requiring no technical skill or knowledge on the part of the operator apart from the ability to change the occasional lamp. Finally, unlike most other projected visuals aids, it requires no room darkening, so that students can take notes throughout the lesson.

Some Basic Guidelines on How to Use the OHP Effectively

Despite its near universal use, many teachers, instructors and trainers fail to get the best out of the overhead projector for various reasons. Many of these relate to the use of the machine itself, since even experienced teachers sometimes fail to observe all the following basic rules:

☐ Position the projector and screen so that the latter can be seen clearly by all the members of the class or group with whom you will be using the machine. In many cases it is best to place the screen in one of the front corners of the room, especially if locating it in a central position would deprive you of access to a fixed chalkboard or markerboard, which you might well find that you want to use in the course of the lesson.

☐ Arrange the projector and screen in such a way as to eliminate or minimize the two forms of keystoning shown in Figure 4.1. The first type arises when the axis of projection is not at right angles to the screen in the horizontal plane, and can be eliminated by placing the projector opposite the centre of the screen. The second type arises in cases when the axis of projection is not at right angles to the screen in the vertical plane, usually because the projection head is too low. It can usually be eliminated or made acceptable by tilting the screen forward (if this is possible). In the case of a fixed vertical screen, the only way to solve the problem may well be to raise the level of the overhead projector itself, provided that this can be done without blocking the learners' view of the screen.

☐ Adjust the distance from the projector to the screen so that the image fills the full area of the latter when properly in focus; failure to use the entire area of the screen can make it difficult for people at the back of the room to make out details.

☐ Make sure that the platen and head lens surfaces are clean and free from dust; dirty or dusty surfaces can reduce image brightness and detract from the clarity and quality of the display.

How to Design and Produce OHP Software

Even if they succeed in getting everything right from a hardware point of view, many overhead projector users do not give sufficient thought to the design of the software that they use or take sufficient care in its preparation to make sure that it achieves the desired objectives. Let us therefore take a systematic look at how the design and production of OHP software should be tackled.

THE TWO BASIC FORMS OF OHP SOFTWARE

First of all, let us take a brief look at the two basic forms that OHP software can take — the continuous roll and the single transparency — and examine their respective uses.

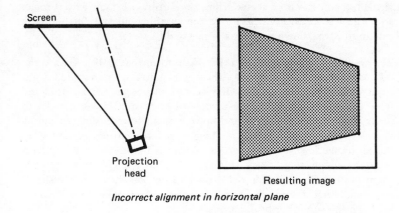

Incorrect alignment in horizontal plane

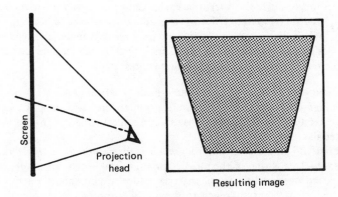

Incorrect alignment in vertical plane

Figure 4.1 **The two causes of keystoning in OHP displays**

The continuous roll: Most overhead projectors are fitted with a system whereby a long roll of acetate film can be wound across the platen from one spool to another. This enables a virtually endless supply of blank film to be used in the course of a lesson, either for writing out a continuous set of notes or for providing a succession of blank surfaces for the display of specific items of material.

Continuous rolls of this type are best suited to the requirements of those who prefer to create their supportive display material during the actual course of a lesson rather than produce it beforehand. They are, for example, the standard display method that is now used by many mathematics lecturers. Beforehand they used to have to write all their material on a chalkboard, which not only entailed their having to rub old material out at regular intervals in order to make room for new material, but also covered their hands and clothes with chalk dust. Now, however, thanks to the advent of the overhead projector with its virtually endless roll of acetate film, they can work their way through an entire lecture without having to rub anything out and, furthermore, can do so sitting down without any messy dust.

The single transparency: The other basic form that OHP software can take is the single transparency, whether mounted or unmounted. Until comparatively recently, most OHP acetate sheets were rather thin and were usually mounted in large cardboard or plastic frames in order to make them easier to handle and prevent them from curling up during use. Now, however, sheets are thicker and less prone to curling up during projection, so that there is no longer the same need to mount them, although some users still prefer to do so. Others simply use them as they are — unmounted — since this makes them much easier to store and carry round, the boxes in which blank sheets are supplied being ideally suited for both purposes.

Although single OHP transparencies can again be used for the creation of display material during the actual course of a lesson, their principal use is in the production of pre-prepared materials. It is with the design and production of such single OHP transparencies that most of the remainder of this section will be concerned.

DESIGNING OHP TRANSPARENCIES — BASIC PRINCIPLES
Although OHP transparencies can be produced in a wide range of forms, there are two basic principles that should underlie the design of all such materials.

First, *do not try to put too much information on a single transparency*. This is one of the most common mistakes that are made when preparing overhead projector materials. Ideally you should restrict the content of each transparency to the presentation of a single concept or limited subject area, using a series of such simple transparencies to cover a complicated topic rather than trying to include everything in a single frame. Remember that including too much detail will not only make the material difficult for the viewers (especially those at the back of the room) to see, but will probably also cause conceptual confusion.

Second, *use a clear, systematic layout*. As with all still visual display materials, the way in which the information is presented is often just as important as the intrinsic content in determining whether the material is effective from an instructional point of view. Thus the material should be laid out clearly and systematically, with any key words or items highlighted in some way (eg by making use of contrasting colours).

PRODUCING THE TRANSPARENCIES
Overhead projector transparencies can be produced by a variety of methods but, whichever method is used, there is one basic rule that overrides all others:

Make sure that all the material will be seen when the transparency is projected. Because most of the blank acetate sheets that are supplied for use with the overhead projector are larger than the effective size of the platen, there is a danger of 'running off the edges' — either vertically or horizontally — unless due care is taken. Also most overhead projectors 'cut the corners' off the image, so any material in the extreme corners of the transparency may well also fail to be seen. Fortunately there is a simple and foolproof way of avoiding all such problems. This involves cutting out a square of thick white card of suitable size (roughly 12 inch square) and marking on the effective limits of the OHP platen using a black marker pen with a reasonably wide point. This should then be used as a work surface and guide during the preparation of all OHP transparencies to be used with the machine in question or machines with the same platen size and shape. The usefulness of such a guide can be further increased by ruling a system of guidelines on its surface using a fine-tipped marker pen. I have found that the best system is a grid of ¼ inch squares, produced by ruling horizontal and vertical lines ¼ inch apart. I have also found it helpful to stick two small pieces of Blu-tack or similar 'rubber adhesive' to the top edge of the card, as shown in Figure 4.2; this enables the acetate sheet to be held firmly in place while you are working on it.

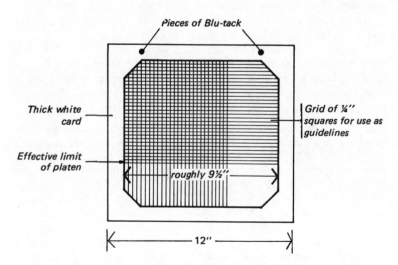

Figure 4.2 **A home-made work surface for the preparation of OHP transparencies**

Producing transparencies by hand: By far the quickest means of producing your own OHP transparencies is to prepare them by hand, using suitable marker pens. Either water-soluble or permanent pens can be used for this purpose, but I strongly recommend the latter since water-soluble material tends to smudge when touched. I find medium-tipped pens best for OHP work, and tend to work with four basic colours —

black, red, blue and green; these are sufficient for most purposes. If large areas of colour are required, these can be added using transfer film, which should be cut to the exact shape required using a scalpel *after* it has been applied to the transparency.

When putting verbal information on OHP transparencies by hand, it is important to use a writing or printing style that all members of the viewing group will be able to read without difficulty. I strongly recommend that you try to develop a clear lower-case printing style for this purpose, since this is generally far easier to decipher than either upper-case printing or ordinary handwriting (see page 43). Also, it is absolutely essential to make the letters big enough to be seen by those furthest from the screen. The recommended sizes for different forms of printing and writing are as follows:

☐ Lower-case printing: just over $1/8$ of an inch (excluding ascenders and descenders).
☐ Upper-case printing: roughly ¼ of an inch.
☐ Handwriting: as for lower-case printing.

It is also advisable to leave a gap of roughly ¼ of an inch between lines and to leave generous spaces between words, since this greatly increases legibility. Thus, use of guidelines ¼ of an inch apart (as recommended in the previous section) can be of considerable help in getting both the size of the lettering and the spacing of the lines right.

It is, of course, also possible to use some form of stencil or template system to add verbal information to OHP transparencies, or even to use instant lettering or machine-generated lettering of some sort if a particularly high-quality finished product is required. For most purposes, however, hand-produced lettering is perfectly adequate and much quicker.

Typing OHP material: Another popular — albeit much abused — method of producing OHP transparencies is to type the material. This can be done either by typing directly on to the acetate sheet using a special ribbon or carbon sheet or by first typing the material on to paper and then making a transparency from this (eg using a thermal copier). It must, however, be stressed that a standard office typewriter should *never* be used for such work since the letters that it produces will always be far too small to be seen clearly when displayed using an overhead projector. A special typewriter (known as a bulletin or primary typewriter) which produces letters roughly twice as large as an ordinary machine should be used for all OHP work.

Producing OHP transparencies from opaque originals: Another standard method of producing OHP transparencies is to use a thermal copier or similar machine to prepare a transparency from an opaque original — eg a page of text. This can produce perfectly acceptable results *provided that the original material is suitable for OHP projection*. As we have seen, ordinary typed material is useless for this purpose and the same is true of most printed materials, since these are normally intended for individual study at close quarters rather than long-range viewing by a group. Thus producing an OHP transparency from (say) a diagram in a book or journal is nearly always worse then useless, since the resulting material will almost invariably be far too small and/or too highly detailed to be seen clearly when projected, especially by the people at the back of the room.

Producing computer-generated OHP materials: In the same way as it is possible to use a word processor or similar computer-based system to create and produce opaque originals for duplication or printing (see page 41), it is now possible to use the computer to design and produce OHP transparencies. The Computer Services Unit at Robert Gordon's Institute of Technology recently acquired such a facility, which can be used to create both alpha-numeric and graphic materials and print them out in overhead transparency form – in full colour, and with whatever size of lettering is wanted. Although it will probably be a long time before machines of this type start to appear in schools, I imagine that they will become standard fixtures in most tertiary education and specialized training establishments in the not too distant future, and will prove to be of enormous help to instructional staff in preparing OHP materials.

The various manual methods of producing OHP transparencies are described in detail in the books by Kemp and by Minor and Frye that are listed in the Bibliography, and interested readers are referred to these.

SOME USEFUL DISPLAY TECHNIQUES
Let us now look at some of the standard techniques that can be used to increase the effectiveness of OHP displays.

Progressive disclosure: This is one of the basic techniques that can be used in overhead projector displays, and one of the most useful from an instructional point of view. It involves covering up all or part of the material on a given transparency, and progressively revealing the material as the presentation proceeds. This has the double advantage of concentrating the mind of the learner on whatever item or section is being discussed at the time and maintaining interest by keeping him in suspense over what is going to be revealed next (a good psychological ploy).

Progressive disclosure can be achieved in a number of ways, the easiest of which is simply to cover the material to be hidden with a sheet of paper, card or other opaque material and then to move it out of the way as and when required. This can be quite effective when used with a simple list of headings or key points, which can be revealed and discussed one by one. There is, however, a tendency for the mask to fall off the projector before the material at the bottom of the transparency is reached, something that can be prevented by weighing it down with a suitable heavy object (eg a bunch of keys or a ruler).

A more sophisticated and more versatile way of achieving progressive disclosure is to cover the various items or sections with individual masks of the required shape and attach these to one or more of the edges of the transparency by means of suitable hinges (eg pieces of Sellotape). The masks can then be pulled back one by one in order to reveal the different items or sections. This technique is particularly useful with graphic displays such as block and flow diagrams, since it enables the various sections of such a diagram to be revealed one by one, thus showing how the complete system is built up. The use of such hinged masks is illustrated in Figure 4.3.

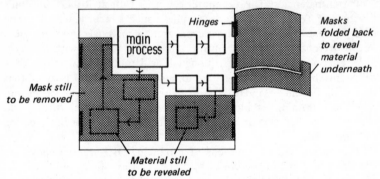

Figure 4.3 **Use of a system of hinged masks to allow progressive disclosure of the various sections of a block diagram**

Use of overlays: Another standard technique that can be used to build up the information content of an overhead projector display is the use of overlays. This differs from progressive disclosure in that the whole of the area of the transparency is revealed from the start, with additional information being added to the original display by superimposing further transparencies on the original. This can be used to guide learners through the development of a complicated display stage by stage, thus avoiding the confusion and/or distraction that might well arise if the entire display were shown right from the start.

There are two basic ways in which material can be overlaid on an OHP display. The first is simply to lay further transparencies, carrying the new information, on top of the first. This may give rise to problems of registration, however, particularly if the display is a complicated one or if exact positioning of the new information is crucial. The second method is to make use of hinged overlays attached to some or all of the edges of the original transparency, overlays that can then be flipped into position as and when required. Use of this system clearly enables the registration problems mentioned above to be avoided, the secret of achieving perfect registration being to add the information to each successive overlay *after* it has been attached to the original transparency and moved into its display position. The way in which a progressively more detailed display can be built up by adding a series of hinged overlays is illustrated in Figure 4.4. Clearly, appropriate use of colours can add greatly to the effectiveness of such a display.

Use of animation: Although the overhead projector is classed as a 'still visual display' system, it is in fact possible to add an element of animation to certain types of OHP display. This can be used to show such things as the flow of fluids along pipes and the direction of flow in flow diagrams. Two basic methods are used to produce such apparent movement. The first is to incorporate special polarizing materials in the display and to add a polarizing spinner to the optical system of the projector, between the platen and the projection head. The second is to make use of moirée fringes to create an illusion of movement in parts of the display. The materials and ancillary equipment needed to produce both types of animation can be obtained from specialist educational suppliers.

PRODUCING TRANSPARENCIES FOR INDIVIDUALIZED STUDY

Although by far the most important use of large transparencies of the type described above is in conjunction with the overhead projector, it is also possible to study them at close quarters using a light box of some sort. Thus such transparencies can be used in individualized study situations as well as in expository and group learning. Transparencies that are primarily intended for such close study rather than for display to a class or group can be produced in exactly the same way as ordinary OHP transparencies. They can, however, be made to incorporate rather more detail, and can also have smaller lettering because of the different conditions under which they are designed to be used.

Photographic Slides and Slide Sequences

Ever since the days of the 'magic lantern', slides have been one of the simplest and most popular methods of introducing supportive visual materials into a lecture or taught lesson. The original 'lantern slides' (which were roughly 3¼ inches square) are very rarely used today, however, having been almost entirely superseded by the newer 'compact' 2 inches x 2 inches slides. These consist of single frames of 35 mm or similar film mounted in cardboard, metal or plastic binders, often between twin sheets of glass for added protection, and are considerably easier to make, handle, use and store than their more cumbersome predecessors — as well as being much cheaper. Such slides can be of considerable assistance to teachers, instructors and trainers of all types in providing visual reinforcement of what is being said, and are particularly useful for showing photographs, diagrams and other graphic material.

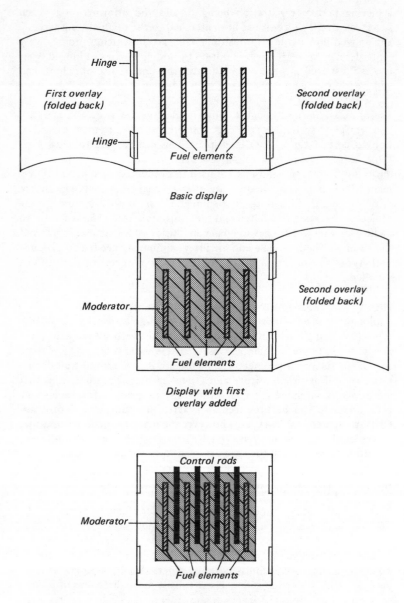

Figure 4.4 Use of a series of overlays to build up a progressively more detailed schematic diagram of the core of a nuclear reactor

The main disadvantage is that they require the room to be darkened, so that students normally cannot take notes while slides are being shown.

Apart from their use as a visual aid in mass instructional and group-learning situations, slides constitute one of the most important media for individualized instruction, usually combined with an audiotape to form a tape-slide (or, more correctly, a slide-tape) programme. This role of slides will be discussed in detail in Chapter 6.

Producing Your Own Slides

There are two main ways in which compact slides can be produced for instructional purposes:

1. Taking photographs of actual scenes, systems, objects, etc.
2. Taking photographs of material carried on other media.

Let us now look at what each of these involves.

PHOTOGRAPHING ACTUAL SCENES, OBJECTS, ETC

To do this, you will need a basic 35 mm camera plus any ancillary equipment that is required for particular types of work (indoor work, close-up work, etc).

The basic camera: Most 35 mm cameras are similar in appearance to the one shown in Figure 4.5, consisting of a camera body to which different types of lens system can be attached. They generally come fitted with a standard 50 mm lens (ie a lens that brings light from a remote object to a focus in a plane 50 mm behind it).

Figure 4.5 **A 35 mm camera fitted with a standard 50 mm lens**

If you are at all serious about producing your own instructional slides, you would probably be best advised to purchase a general-purpose camera of semi-professional quality, costing something of the order of £150-£200 at today's (ie 1985) prices. If you spend much less than this, the camera will almost certainly lack some of the facilities that you will require, while if you spend much more, it will probably be too sophisticated for the type of work you will be carrying out.

Additional lenses that you will probably need: Although the standard 50 mm lens that is fitted to your basic camera may well enable you to take the great majority of the shots that you require, you will probably find it useful to have a number of alternative lenses available for specific shots. For most purposes, the following should be sufficient.

☐ A wide-angle lens (cost roughly £50), for increasing the field of view obtainable from a given position.
☐ A zoom or telephoto lens (cost roughly £90), to enable you to photograph a specific part of a scene in detail or magnify remote objects.

If you have to carry out close-up photography of really small objects, however, you will probably find that you also require a set of lens extension tubes (cost roughly £25). These enable the standard 50 mm lens to be converted into close-up lenses suitable for work at different fixed distances. Indeed, if you have to carry out a lot of work of this type, you may well find it advisable to purchase a close-up bellows and bellow lens system (cost roughly £100), which will enable you to work at any distance simply by adjusting the bellows (see Figure 4.6).

Other equipment required: Although the camera can be hand-held for most shots, there will undoubtedly be occasions when you will find it advisable to mount it on a tripod − especially for close-up work. A standard tripod can be obtained for around £30.

If you intend working indoors, you will also require some form of artificial lighting. The simplest way to provide such light is to use an electronic flash system (cost around £20-£25), but there may well also be situations where you will find that it is necessary to use floodlights. A reasonably good pair of tungsten lamps, with stands, can be purchased for around £75-£100 and will probably be sufficient for most purposes.

Armed with the above equipment and a supply of suitable film, you should find that it is possible to produce satisfactory photographic slides of virtually any scene, system or object − outdoors or indoors. Further guidance can be obtained from any basic text on photography (eg the one by Langford listed in the Bibliography).

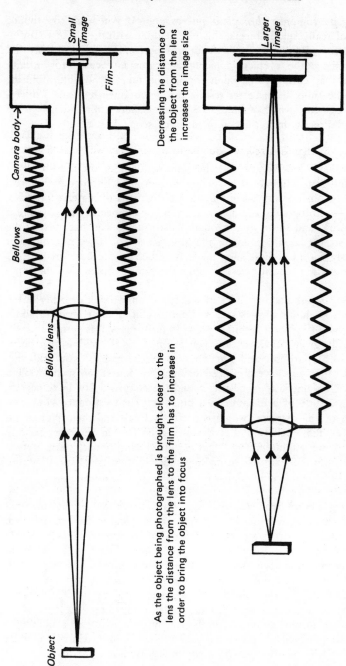

Decreasing the distance of the object from the lens increases the image size

As the object being photographed is brought closer to the lens the distance from the lens to the film has to increase in order to bring the object into focus

Figure 4.6 Use of a bellows and bellow lens to photograph small objects at different distances

Taking photographs through a microscope: If you want to produce slides of really small objects, this can be done with the aid of an ordinary microscope. Simply focus the microscope on the object visually and then remove the eyepiece, placing the camera (focused for infinite distance) as close to the open top of the tube as possible, pointing down the tube. Even better results can be obtained by using a microscope adaptor, which enables a 35 mm camera (minus lens) to be screwed directly on to the end of the microscope draw tube.

PRODUCING SLIDES FROM OTHER MEDIA

It is probably true to say that the great majority of the slides that are used for instructional purposes are not original photographs of real scenes or objects but 'second-hand' photographs of material on other media — photographs and diagrams from books, specially prepared text or artwork, and so on. It is probably also true to say that most of the slides so prepared are made illegally, since the laws of copyright expressly forbid copies being made of other people's material (other than in certain special cases) without the prior permission of the copyright holder.

Thus, before making slides of material from a book or other publication, you should always seek the permission of the copyright holder if you wish to remain within the law. In most cases, this permission will be readily given provided that you are making the slides for genuine educational purposes and not for commercial gain. If you are using material that you have produced yourself, of course, no such problem arises. Thus one way of getting round the copyright law in respect of making a slide of a diagram in a book (say) is to produce your own version of the diagram (which is perfectly legal) and then photograph this. You may well find that this is a good idea in any case, because much of the graphic material that is published in books, journals etc is totally unsuitable for use in making slides in its original form because it contains too much detail, has too small lettering, and so on.

Preparing material for slide-making: When preparing original material for slide-making, whether it is textual or graphical in nature, the same basic rules as were stated earlier for OHP transparencies (see p 98) apply — only more so. Thus you should *never* try to put too much information on a single slide, and should always aim to produce a clear, simple lay-out that will enable all the information on the slide to be distinguishable by the viewer. This is particularly important if the slide is to be shown to a large group of people, or projected in a large room. If you are in any doubt about the clarity or legibility of a slide once you have produced it, go to the back of the room in which it is to be shown and see whether you have any difficulty in deciphering it.

When preparing the artwork for slides that are to carry verbal information, a good rule of thumb is to restrict yourself to a maximum of six lines of print if the slide is to be screened horizontally and eight if it is to be screened vertically. (Vertical format slides are not recommended, however, because most screens are designed to show horizontal slides; thus, if the projector is arranged so as to fill the screen with such slides, any vertical format slides shown will be 'topped and tailed' — much to the annoyance of viewers.) The easiest way to produce the artwork for such textual slides is to type it in a rectangle roughly 8 cm x 6 cm. This will produce artwork with the correct aspect ratio (ratio of horizontal to vertical size) and will also produce lettering of a suitable size for distant viewing. Use of a modern electric typewriter to produce the artwork generally produces satisfactory results; this should be set at double the normal spacing in order to increase the clarity of the text.

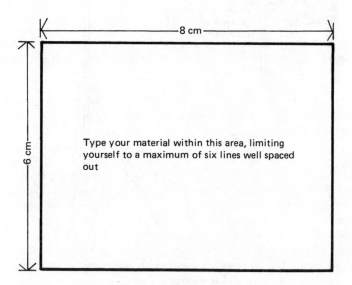

Figure 4.7 **The frame within which textual material for 35 mm slides should be typed**

Photographing the material: In order to make photographic slides from opaque originals, it is essential to use some sort of rigid mounting system for the camera; holding the camera by hand simply does not produce satisfactory results.

There are two basic techniques that can be used for such copy work. The first — and simplest — is to place the material to be copied on a support stand of some sort and to mount the camera on a tripod — preferably one with a pan/tilt head in order to allow it to be angled downwards. If the artwork is then illuminated using a pair of suitable lamps, as shown in Figure 4.8, it is possible to produce satisfactory slides by this method.

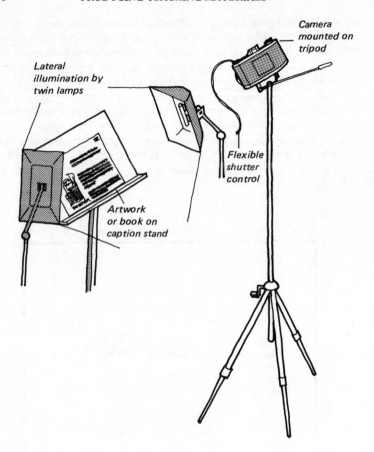

Figure 4.8 **Use of a caption stand and tripod-mounted camera for making slides**

Although the caption stand and tripod method is perfectly satisfactory for occasional use, anyone who intends to make large numbers of slides from opaque material would probably be advised to buy or make some sort of copy stand, since the use of such a system makes the work much easier. If you have the necessary funds, it is possible to buy a complete copy stand system of whatever sophistication you require, but such systems tend to be rather expensive, so that their purchase can probably only be justified if you have a very large throughput indeed. It is, however, a relatively simple matter to construct a rudimentary copy stand that is satisfactory for most purposes. Basically, all that is needed is a vertical column of some sort to which the camera can be fixed so that it can be moved up and down directly above the material to be copied and a system of lamps whereby the latter can be illuminated without producing reflected glare (lamps angled at 45° to the vertical are best). Such a set-up is shown in Figure 4.9.

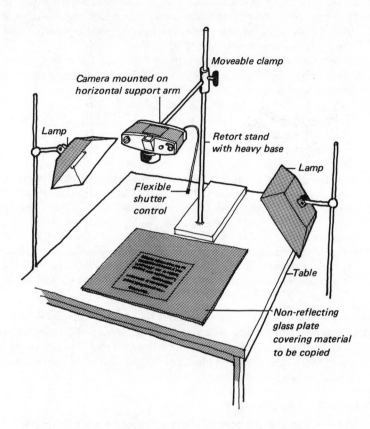

Figure 4.9 **A 'do-it-yourself' copy stand system**

Producing slides from computer-generated material: As we saw earlier, it is now possible to use a computer to design and produce overhead projector transparencies (see p 101). By using appropriate ancillary equipment, it is possible to use the same system to produce photographic slides, a facility that will again undoubtedly become increasingly widely used in the tertiary education and training sectors in future years. Indeed, use of the computer to generate original visual material for display using other media could well become *the* main source of production of such material in establishments which are able to acquire the necessary facilities.

THE DIFFERENT TYPES OF 35 mm FILM AND THEIR MAIN
APPLICATIONS
There are four main types of 35 mm film, all of which have different

applications.

1. *Colour negative film*: this is the type of film that is used when the final product is to take the form of colour prints, the prints being produced in whatever size is required using a suitable enlarger; such film is not normally used for making slides.
2. *Colour reversal film*: the main type of film used for making colour slides, with the film that is used to take the photograph being reversed from a negative to a positive during processing.
3. *Panchromatic monochrome film*: monochrome film that is sensitive to the entire visible spectrum. Its main use is in preparing negatives for eventual conversion into monochrome prints, but it can also be processed through to the positive stage in order to produce positive monochrome slides.
4. *Line film:* special monochrome film that is used for photographing line originals which possess no half tones. Slides produced using such film have the image in white against a black background, but the lines can be coloured using special photographic dye if required. Line negatives are also used in the production of diazo slides, which are made from such negatives by a secondary process (involving ammonia fumes) in which the image is transferred to diazo film. The resulting slides have a white image on a coloured background (usually blue).

There are in fact several other processes by which photographic slides can be produced, but discussion of these is beyond the scope of an introductory book of this nature. Information on such processes can be found in specialized books on photography (see, for example, the book on *Basic Photography* listed in the Bibliography).

PREPARING SLIDES FOR USE

Once a roll of 35 mm film has been exposed, it is obviously necessary to process the film before it can be used. The easiest way to do this is to pay to have the film processed in a commercial laboratory, although this inevitably causes a considerable time lag between taking the pictures and being able to use them. If you have the necessary skills and facilities, or have access to a photographic processing service 'in-house', such delays can obviously be avoided, although the final cost of the slides may in fact turn out to be higher than if you had them processed externally once you have taken labour and cost of materials into account.

If you have slides processed by a commercial organization, they will almost invariably be returned to you in cardboard mounts, without glass. If the slides are to be subjected to heavy use, however, it will probably pay you in the long run to remove the transparencies from these mounts (by slitting the latter open with a scalpel or razor blade) and re-mount them in plastic or metal mounts, preferably between glass. This will not only protect them from damage, but will also prevent them from popping or buckling during projection. If you are processing the slides yourself or having them processed 'in-house', they should be mounted in this way right from the start.

The final thing that has to be done before the slides are ready for use is spotting and labelling. In order to ensure that a slide is always inserted into a projector or viewer the right way round and right way up, a spot should be stuck or marked on the bottom left-hand corner of the front of the slide (ie the side from which the image appears right way round when the slide is held up to the light). When the slide is subsequently loaded into a projector, this spot should always appear at the top right-hand corner when viewed from behind the projector (since the image on a slide is inverted and laterally reversed during projection, the slide has to be turned through 180^0 about an axis perpendicular to its surface before being loaded if it is to appear right way up when projected). When the slide is loaded into a 'straight through' magnifying viewer, on the other hand, the spot should be on the bottom left-hand corner.

Labelling of slides (essential if confusion is to be avoided during subsequent storage and use) is best carried out by sticking a self-adhesive slide label along the bottom or top edge and writing on this. Such labels often incorporate a spot at one end so, by sticking them on the bottom edge, separate spotting is made unnecessary.

Duplicating Slides

If more than one copy of a slide is needed, and this is known before the original photographic work is carried out, it is obviously a good idea to shoot as many copies of the slide as are required right at the outset. This will ensure that all the copies are of the same high standard. Should additional copies become necessary after the photography has been completed, however, these can be produced either by having duplicate slides made by a commercial laboratory or by carrying out the duplication yourself. Such duplication can be carried out in two ways.

1. *The projection method*: This involves projecting the slide on to a screen and photographing the resulting image using a camera mounted as close to the axis of projection as possible; some loss of colour and increase in contrast is inevitable, however, during the process.
2. *The transmission method*: This involves mounting the slide in front of a suitable source of light and making a direct copy using a camera fitted with a suitable lens extension tube or bellows so that 1 : 1 size focusing can be obtained. This generally produces much more satisfactory results than the projection method, especially if a custom-designed slide duplication unit is used.

Storing Slides

Although slides can, at a pinch, be stored in the small boxes in which they are received from the processing laboratory or in empty slide mount boxes, a more convenient and systematic method is advisable if large numbers are involved. Possible alternatives include the following:

☐ Use of custom-designed slide cabinets, in which the slides are held in individual slots or between moveable partitions in drawers. This is a reasonably inexpensive method, but one that requires an individual slide to be removed from the storage system before it can be inspected.

☐ Use of transparent hanging files fitted with slide pockets. Another inexpensive method that enables the slides to be stored in a standard filing cabinet and also enables an entire sheet of slides to be viewed at the same time (by holding it up to the light or placing it on a light box).

☐ Use of a storage display cabinet, in which the slides are stored on open vertical or horizontal racks which can be slid out in front of an in-built light source for inspection. This is by far the best method, if you can afford the relatively high price of such a cabinet; the one shown in Figure 4.10 can hold up to 3000 slides, arranged in racks of 100, and can be used both for storage and for sorting slides into sequence.

Figure 4.10 A slide storage display cabinet being used for slide sorting

Planning and Using Slide Sequences

Although individual slides can be of considerable use in providing visual back-up material during a lecture or taught lesson, it is generally more effective to employ them in carefully planned linked sequences. When planning and using such sequences, I have always found the following general guidelines useful.

☐ Plan your sequence of slides in such a way that it gives a logical structure to your presentation, using title slides at the start of each major section and subsection; these will not only serve as useful 'signposts' for your audience, but will also help to cue you into each section.

☐ Within each section, use the slides to illustrate and reinforce the points that you want to make, preferably using a fresh slide for each new point covered.

☐ Make sure that the slide that is on display at any given time is relevant to what is being said — if it is not, it may well distract the listeners; if necessary, make use of blank slides (ie slides with dark fields) to cover any sections where no suitable slides are available.

☐ Prepare your sequence of slides for use by laying them out, in order of showing, on a light box or in a rack of a slide storage display cabinet. Transfer them into the slide projector magazine in complete sections.

☐ If at all possible, use a magazine with sufficient capacity to hold all the slides in your presentation; if there are too many for one magazine, change magazines at the end of a major section — *not* right in the middle of a continuous sequence.

☐ Use a projector with a remote change facility, and make sure that the cable to the hand control is long enough to enable you to give your presentation from the front of the group that you are talking to, and also to enable you to move about if necessary.

☐ Remember that your audience will not be able to take notes during your presentation; thus, if you want them to have a permanent record of what is covered, prepare a suitable handout to support your lecture or lesson.

The use of slide sequences in individualized instruction will be discussed in Chapter 6.

Bibliography

Anderson, R H (1976) *Selecting and Developing Media for Instruction*. Van Nostrand Reinhold, Cincinnati (Chapters 4 and 5).

Kemp, J E (1980) *Planning and Producing Audiovisual Materials*. Harper and Row Publishers Inc, New York.

Langford, M J (1973) *Basic Photography*. Focal Press, London and New York.

Langford, M J (1973) *Visual Aids and Photography in Education*. Focal

Press, London and New York.

Minor, E and Frye, H R (1970) *Techniques for Producing Visual Instructional Media*. McGraw Hill, New York.

Romiszowski, A J (1974) *The Selection and Use of Instructional Media*. Kogan Page, London (Chapter 4).

Rowatt, R W (1980) *A Guide to the Use of the Overhead Projector*. Scottish Council for Educational Technology, Glasgow.

Vincent, A (1970) *The Overhead Projector*. Educational Foundation for Visual Aids, London.

Wittich, W A and Schuller, C F (1979) *Instructional Technology — Its Nature and Use*. Harper and Row, New York.

Chapter 5
How to Produce Audio Materials

Introduction

Having completed our examination of the three main classes of still visual display materials that can be used by teachers and trainers, we will now take a look at a completely different type of medium — audio materials. In their own way, these have had just as great an impact on instructional methodology as any of the visual media discussed so far and, as we shall see in Chapter 6, are also a key component of some of the most important linked audio and visual systems developed to date.

Following our established pattern, we will begin by taking a general look at how audio materials in general, and audiotapes in particular, can be used in different types of instructional situation. Next we will take a fairly detailed look at the basic principles of audio recording and editing. Finally, we will offer guidance on how to design audio materials for specific instructional purposes, including audiotapes for individual and class use and materials for language laboratories.

How Audio Materials can be used in Different Teaching/Learning Situations

As in the case of still display materials, audio materials can be used in virtually all types of teaching/learning situations, covering all three of the basic classes identified earlier. Let us therefore see what basic roles they are capable of playing in each.

Mass Instruction

Here we can identify at least three highly important roles for audio materials. The first is as a source of supportive and illustrative material for use in expository teaching — recorded music, poems and plays, recorded extracts from talks and speeches, foreign languages spoken by native speakers, and so on. Such materials can be used in all situations where an audio input of some sort would increase the effectiveness of the instructional process — or simply help to maintain student interest and concentration by varying the method of presentation.

The second way in which audio materials can be used is as the actual

117

vehicle by which the mass instruction is carried out. Examples of such mediated instruction include the various types of educational radio broadcast, either used 'off-air' or recorded on audiotape for use at a more convenient time or more appropriate stage in the curriculum, and the wide range of pre-recorded lessons and lectures that are available on record or audiotape. Self-contained 'audio lessons' of this type — and similar lessons produced 'in-house' by a teacher or instructor — can, on occasions, be a highly effective substitute for a live exposition.

The third main method of using audio materials in mass instructional situations is as a vehicle for enactive learning of some sort. Examples include the use of tape recorders to record simulated interviews, debates, scenes from plays, musical performances, and so on for subsequent replay, discussion or criticism. Other examples include the use of audio materials in language laboratories and similar 'electronic classroom' situations.

Individualized Instruction

If anything, audio materials are capable of playing an even more important role in individualized instruction than in mass instruction, either on their own or in conjunction with visual media of various types. Here they can be used in at least three basic ways. The first is as a vehicle for conveying the actual content of the instruction to the learner, with the learner having a more-or-less passive role and merely having to listen to the material. Most educational radio broadcasts fall into this class, as do many self-instructional audiotapes and records. The second is as a means of managing the instructional process, with the audio material (usually an audiotape) acting as a sort of 'talking study guide' that is used in conjunction with other materials such as textbooks, notes and worksheets. The third is similar to the third role described in the 'mass instruction' section, with the audio materials providing a vehicle for enactive learning in which the learner actually has to interact with the materials themselves. Most self-instructional systems for learning foreign languages fall into this last category, with the audio material being supplied on a gramophone record or audiotape.

Group Learning

Audio materials can also play a useful role in many types of group-learning activity. They can be used in three basic ways:

1. As a vehicle for supplying information to the group, either of an illustrative or supportive nature or as part of the main content of the exercise.
2. As a vehicle for managing or guiding the group through the exercise.
3. By providing a vehicle with or through which the members of the group have to interact.

The Basic Principles of Sound Recording and Editing

Of the main purely audio media (radio, gramophone records and audio-tapes), the only one where it is practical for teachers, instructors and trainers to produce their own materials is the last. We will therefore devote the remainder of this chapter to the production of audiotapes, beginning by taking a fairly detailed look at the basics of audio recording and editing and then showing how to produce audiotape materials for specific instructional purposes.

How Sound is Recorded on Audiotape

The various processes that take place in audiotape recording and play-back are shown schematically in Figures 5.1 and 5.2 respectively.

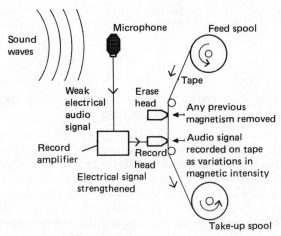

Figure 5.1 **Schematic representation of the various stages of audiotape recording**

In the recording process, the first stage takes place in the microphone. Here the incident sound waves cause a membrane of some sort to vibrate, and these mechanical vibrations are converted into a weak electrical signal whose amplitude follows the amplitude of the original sound exactly (a so-called analogue signal). Next, the electrical signal is passed into the record amplifier of the tape recorder, where it is increased in strength and, in most cases, also has its high frequencies artificially enhanced in order to increase the signal-to-noise ratio in the final recording. The signal is then fed into the record head, an electro-magnet that produces between its poles a magnetic field whose intensity varies in exactly the same way as the amplitude of the electrical sound signal. The recording tape is coated with a thin layer of magnetizable iron oxide or chromium oxide powder and, as it passes across the narrow gap between the poles of the record head magnet, has the signal recorded on its surface in the form of a weak magnetic field with the same intensity profile as the original sound.

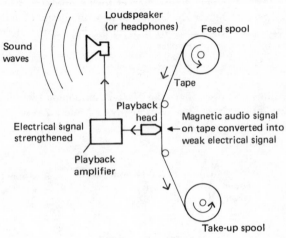

Figure 5.2 **Schematic representation of the various stages of audiotape playback**

In the playback process, exactly the opposite chain of transformations takes place. First, the tape moves across the surface of the playback head, an electro-magnet with a similar structure to the record head. Here the variations in magnetic intensity as the tape crosses the gap of the head cause a weak electrical signal to be induced within the head. This is then passed into the playback amplifier, where it has its strength greatly increased, and also has any artificial boosting of the high frequencies that was introduced during the recording stage removed. The electrical signal is then passed into a loudspeaker, where it is converted into mechanical vibrations of the loudspeaker cone. These, in turn, produce sound waves that are (in a high-quality system) more or less an exact reproduction of the original sound that struck the microphone. Alternatively, the electrical signal can be fed into a set of headphones, which are simply two miniature loudspeakers designed for individual listening.

Equipment Needed for Audiotape Recording

To record material on audiotape, you require two basic items of equipment: a microphone and a tape recorder. Let us now look at the various types that are available.

MICROPHONES

Microphones come in a wide range of types and, like most other items of audiovisual hardware, vary enormously in quality and price. Thus, when buying a microphone, it is important to choose one that is of a suitable type to do the job that you have in mind and is also of a quality that matches the rest of your equipment. Clearly, buying a cheap, low-fidelity microphone for use with an expensive, high-fidelity tape recorder is a false economy, since any audio system is only as good as its weakest link. Conversely, there is no point in buying an expensive microphone for use with a cheap tape recorder that will not be able to do justice to the signal that it produces. For most purposes, a microphone costing about £20 is perfectly adequate.

Microphones differ both in terms of the basic physical principle on which they operate and in terms of their directional characteristics. With regard to the former, there are three main types in common use.

☐ *Crystal or ceramic microphones*, in which the transducer (the mechanism that converts mechanical vibrations into an electrical signal) consists of a piezo-electric crystal or a layer of piezo-electric ceramic granules. Such microphones are cheap but are not very rugged, have a limited frequency range, and produce only a low-fidelity signal; they are the sort that are built into many low-cost cassette recorders.

☐ *Moving coil (dynamic) microphones*, in which the transducer is a coil of wire that moves between the poles of the magnet. Such microphones have a wider frequency response than crystal or ceramic microphones, and also produce a higher quality signal; they are, however, more expensive.

☐ *Capacitor (condenser) microphones*, in which the transducer is a capacitor of variable gap that produces an electrical signal when one of its plates vibrates in response to incident sound. Such microphones have an even wider frequency response than dynamic microphones, and produce high-quality signals; they can also be made extremely small.

☐ With regard to the different directional qualities of microphones, we can distinguish four main types:

☐ *Omni-directional microphones*, which are equally sensitive in all directions when suitably mounted. These are suitable for recording group discussions and in other situations where the sound comes from all directions.

☐ *Bi-directional* (or *figure of eight*) *microphones*, which are sensitive in two opposite horizontal directions but not in directions at right angles to these. These are suitable for recording interviews involving two people, with one on either side of the microphone.

☐ *Cardioid microphones*, which are highly sensitive in one direction, less sensitive in directions at right angles to this, and not sensitive at all in the opposite direction. These are suitable for recording a single speaker, a choir, or any other sound source where the sound

effectively comes from a single direction.
☐ *Gun* (or *rifle*) *microphones*, which are highly directional in their sensitivity, only picking up sound within a narrow cone. These are suitable for picking up sound from a single source located some distance away.

The differing directional properties of these four types are shown in Figure 5.3, which shows polar diagrams of their sensitivity in different directions.

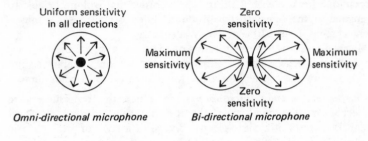

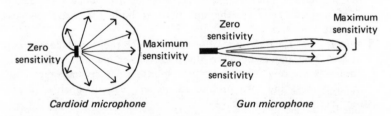

Figure 5.3 **Polar response diagrams of different types of microphone**

TAPE RECORDERS

These are of two basic types: open-reel recorders and cassette recorders. The former make use of detachable open reels as feed and take-up spools, and generally the tape has to be threaded manually through the tape head and drive mechanisms before use. The latter make use of sealed tape cassettes that contain both the feed and take-up spools, and are loaded simply by fitting the cassette into place in the machine. Apart from this, however, the two types of recorder work in exactly the same way, and can be used to do more or less the same things.

The other main way in which the tape recorders differ is in terms of the track configuration of the tapes that they use. In the case of open-reel machines, there are five main configurations that you are likely to come across. These are shown schematically in Figure 5.4. In all cases, the tape is ¼ of an inch wide.

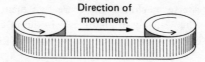

Full-track monophonic: only one recording track, covering virtually the entire width of the tape, so that such tapes cannot be turned over in order to record on 'the other side'. (Note: this system is only used in highly expensive tape recorders of 'broadcast' quality — the type that are used by professional sound engineers and broadcasters.)

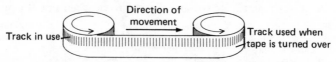

Half-track monophonic: two recording tracks, one on each half of the tape, with only one being used at a time; reversing the tape (ie turning it round so that the take-up spool becomes the feed spool) brings the other track into use. (This is the system that is used in most high-quality single-channel audio work.)

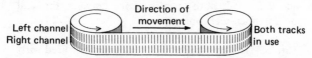

Half-track (two-track) stereophonic: two recording tracks, with one being used to record each channel of a stereophonic signal (or separate signals).

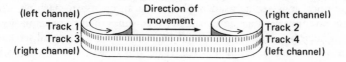

Quarter track (four track) stereophonic: four recording tracks, with tracks 1 and 3 being used when the tape is used as shown and tracks 2 and 4 being used when it is turned over.

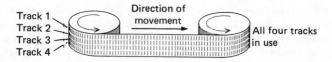

Multi-track: four or more separate tracks, each used to carry a separate sound signal.

Figure 5.4 **The five main track configurations used with open-reel audio tape recorders**

In the case of cassette machines, there are two main configurations. These are shown schematically in Figure 5.5. In the case of the compact cassettes that are now almost universally used, the tape is 4 mm wide.

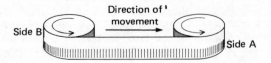

Monophonic: two recording tracks, one on each half of the tape, with the bottom track shown in the figure being used when side A of the cassette is used and the top track when side B is used.

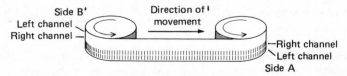

Quarter-track (four-track) stereophonic: four recording tracks, with the bottom two tracks shown in the figure being used when side A of the cassette is used and the top two tracks being used when side B is used; note the difference between this and the corresponding open-reel configuration.

Figure 5.5 **The two main track configurations used with compact cassette recorders**

When choosing a tape recorder for a particular response, you should be aware of these different track configurations and select a machine that is capable of doing the job you have in mind. For making original recordings, it is strongly advisable to use an open-reel machine, since these not only produce better quality recordings than cassette machines of a similar price but also make editing much easier, as we will see later. Unless you have to produce material of 'broadcast' standard (in which case you will have to invest something of the order of £1500 in a full-track machine), you will probably find that a half-track monophonic recorder costing roughly £200 is perfectly adequate for most purposes. For making master tapes, either an open-reel or cassette machine may be used, but it is again important to choose one of reasonable quality, otherwise fidelity will be lost during the transfer process. If you already have a good open-reel machine, it would probably be best to buy a general-purpose four-track stereophonic cassette recorder for this purpose, preferably one with pulsing facilities, so that you can use it for tape-slide work. Such a machine can again be obtained for around £200. For playing a recording back to a class or group, it is again advisable to use a machine of reasonably high quality — preferably one with an external loudspeaker, since machines with built-in speakers can be difficult to hear clearly from the back of a room. When choosing machines for individual use, on the other hand, cheap monophonic cassette players (costing as little as £20 each) may well be all that is required, since quality of reproduction is normally not nearly so important when tapes — particularly ones carrying spoken material — are being listened to through headphones. Such machines can be used to play both monophonic and stereophonic tapes. With the latter, the mono head simply picks up the signals from the two stereo tracks (which occupy the same area as a mono track) and reproduce them as a single combined signal.

THE DIFFERENT TYPES OF TAPE

The magnetic tape used in audio recording consists of an insulating base material (usually some form of plastic, mylar or polyester) coated with a thin layer of magnetizable powder. In most tapes, the latter consists of particles of ferrous oxide, but some high-quality tapes use the more expensive chromium dioxide, since this produces less background noise (tape hiss) and gives a higher sound output level and a higher fidelity recording. Most high-quality tape recorders incorporate a switch that enables circuits suitable for use with the two different types of tape to be selected.

In the case of open-reel tapes, three different grades of tape are available: standard or 1.5 mil tape (tape with a thickness of 1.5 thousandths of an inch), long-play or 1.0 mil tape, and extra long-play or 0.5 mil tape. Clearly, the length of tape that can be wound on a spool of a given size (and hence the playing time at a given speed) depends on this thickness, with a 1.0 mil tape giving 50 per cent more playing time than a 1.5 mil tape on a reel of the same size and a 0.5 mil tape giving 100 per cent more. On the other hand, thicker tapes produce better-quality recordings with less print through (unwanted transfer of the signal from one layer of the tape to the next), and also tend to last longer. Thus, it is advisable to use 1.5 mil tapes for original and master recordings, although 1.0 mil tape can be used in the case of long programmes. 0.5 mil tape is not recommended for high-quality work; indeed, some tape recorders cannot handle such tape at all.Figure 5.6 shows the playing times that are available with different sizes of spool of the three thicknesses of tape at different tape speeds (measured in inches per second). Note that these times are for one pass of the tape only, and should be doubled if both sides of the tape are used.

In the case of compact cassettes, the cassette is designated with a number that shows its total playing time in minutes if both sides are used. The most common sizes are as follows:

C 30 — playing time 15 min. per side.
C 45 — playing time 22½ min. per side.
C 60 — playing time 30 min. per side.
C 90 — playing time 45 min. per side.
C 120 — playing time 60 min. per side.

Type of tape	Diameter of reel (inches)	Length of tape (feet)	Playing time at 7½ ips	Playing time at 3¾ ips
Standard	5	600	15 min.	30 min.
(1.5 mil)	7	1200	30 min.	60 min.
Long-play	5	900	22½ min.	45 min.
(1.0 mil)	7	1800	45 min.	90 min.
Extra-long play	5	1200	30 min.	60 min.
(0.5 mil)	7	2400	60 min.	120 min.

Figure 5.6 **Playing times for different types and lengths of open-reel tape**

As in the case of open-reel tapes, the thickness of the tape in cassettes with very long playing times is less than for shorter-play cassettes, with an associated reduction both in quality and in durability. Indeed, C120 tape is so thin that it tends to jam many machines, and is not recommended for instructional use.

One final word of warning about buying tapes. It is seldom advisable to try to economize by buying cheap tapes, since these not only produce a lower quality of recording and are, in many cases, prone to jamming, but can also cause excessive wear and fouling up of the recorder heads. Thus, always buy good-quality tapes from a reputable supplier; it will pay you in the long run.

How to Make a Recording

The way in which you set about making a recording on audiotape will obviously depend to a large extent on the nature of the material to be recorded and the purpose for which it is to be used. There are, however, some general rules that should always be observed.

1. *Make sure that what you are recording is of the highest possible quality*
   This is a fairly obvious point, but one that is all too often neglected. In most cases, the key to producing high-quality original material is careful preparation, both in terms of planning and writing the materials and in terms of making sure that the presenter(s) or performer(s) are thoroughly briefed and rehearsed. If you are recording spoken material, it is also important to use a presenter with a good, clear delivery — preferably someone who has had training in and/or experience of such work. If at all possible, I strongly recommend the use of a professional presenter (eg an obliging local radio announcer) for any particularly important recording work, since this can make a tremendous difference to the quality of the final product.

2. *Try to optimize the recording environment*
   If you want to produce a good-quality recording, it is essential to carry out the recording work in a suitable environment. First (and most important) it *must* be free from extraneous noise. Remember that a human listener automatically 'filters out' unwanted background noise by concentrating exclusively on what he wants to hear, but that a tape recorder does not, faithfully recording every sound that falls on its microphone. Thus, background noise that is hardly noticed at the time a recording is being made can prove intolerable when the resulting recording is played back. Second, the environment should have appropriate acoustic properties, being neither too reverberant (as in a swimming pool) nor too 'dead' (as in a heavily carpeted and curtained room full of soft furniture). If you are not sure whether the environment is satisfactory, carry out a trial recording and, if something is obviously wrong, try to improve matters by judicious use of acoustic screens, absorbent materials, and so on. Even a few coats hung in strategic positions round a microphone can sometimes make all the difference, as can the siting of the microphone in an open-ended box lined with absorbent materials such as felt or foam rubber. In some cases, of course, it may be better to move to a completely different location, eg by recording narrative material in a quiet room at home rather than trying to compete with the inevitable background noise that is present in most working environments.

3. *Use appropriate equipment and materials*
   This, of course, is fundamental, for if you use inappropriate equipment or unsuitable tape, the resulting recording will invariably turn out to be not as good as it might be. Thus, you should always:

   ☐ Use an external microphone (*not* one built into the tape recorder) of sufficient quality to do justice to the rest of the equipment — preferably one with directional properties suitable for the job you want it to do (an omni-directional microphone for group work, a bi-directional microphone for interviews, a cardioid microphone for a single speaker or uni-directional sound source, and so on).

   ☐ Use the best tape recorder available, assuming it is suitable for the job in hand and bearing in mind that open-reel machines are generally much more suitable for making original recordings than cassette machines.

   ☐ Use a good quality tape of suitable grade and of sufficient length to give the required playing time at the tape speed you intend using.

4. *Get the most out of your equipment and materials*
   Even if you buy the finest recording equipment on the market, you will only obtain good results if you use the equipment correctly. Thus, if you want to get the most out of your equipment and materials, you should:

☐ Select a tape speed that is sufficiently high to produce the quality of recording you require. With compact cassette recorders, the tape speed is fixed (at $1\frac{7}{8}$ ips), but with open-reel machines, it can be set at various values (usually $1\frac{7}{8}$ ips, $3\frac{3}{4}$ ips, $7\frac{1}{2}$ ips and 15 ips). With such machines, the quality of the resulting recording increases as the tape speed increases, especially in terms of high-frequency response, so you should always make sure that this speed is high enough to produce satisfactory results. When recording speech, you will probably find that one of the lower speeds is perfectly adequate, but you will probably have to use a higher speed when recording music if you want the fidelity of the recording to be high. Also, you will probably find that you need to employ higher tape speeds with older tape recorders than with more modern machines; the latter have smaller gaps in their heads, and thus give a better frequency response at a given tape speed.

☐ Set the recording level correctly. Some machines have a facility that allows this level to be controlled automatically, but this should *never* be used when recording speech or any other material that has periods of silence; during such quiet periods, the machine increases the gain of its input amplifier in order to try to bring the signal strength up to the required level, thus causing the background noise level to increase sharply. To prevent this, the recording level should always be set manually, using the relevant meter(s) or indicator(s) for guidance (these are incorporated in all but the cheapest machines). In most cases, the best setting is to have the average level just below the 'overload' area, so that the level only enters this area during peaks (see Figure 5.7). If the level is much lower than this, the recorded signal will be too weak; if it is higher, you will probably find that the peaks are distorted.

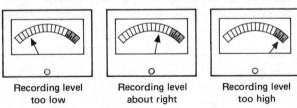

Recording level too low   Recording level about right   Recording level too high

Figure 5.7 **How to set the recording level**

☐ Use the 'pause' control for starting and stopping the tape during recording rather than the 'play' and 'stop' controls. Use of the latter almost invariably introduces unpleasant clicks and other forms of transient distortion into the recording, whereas use of the 'pause' control is (in the case of a good recorder) virtually unnoticeable.

How to Edit Tapes

Once material has been recorded on audiotape, it is often necessary to carry out some form of editing before the tape can be used, eg in order to remove bad takes, coughs and other unwanted sections, to insert pauses, or to rearrange the material in a different order. Such editing can be carried out in two ways: by physically cutting up and rejoining the tape (mechanical editing) and by dubbing the signal from one tape to another (electronic editing). Let us examine the two methods in turn.

MECHANICAL EDITING

Clearly, this form of editing can only be carried out on an open-reel tape (hence one of the reasons for using open-reel machines for original recording work), and only on tapes that carry a single recorded track. It is also much easier to carry out on tapes that are recorded at a fairly high tape speed.

The method involves listening carefully to the recorded tape, noting the approximate positions where cuts have to be made with the aid of the index counter on the recorder. The exact position of each cut should then be found by moving the tape manually backwards and forwards through the playback head and marking its position on the tape using a felt pen or chinagraph pencil. The final cutting and re-joining should be made using a tape splicing block, a cradle of non-ferrous metal that holds the ends of the tape precisely in position during the cutting and splicing process. The various stages in the process are shown in Figure 5.8.

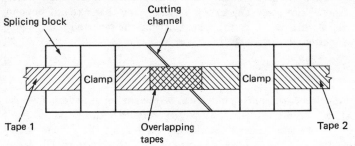

Stage 1 Clamp the two pieces of tape to be joined in the splicing block, base (ie shiny) side up, so that they just overlap across the 45^0 cutting channel.

Figure 5.8 **How to splice two lengths of audiotape together**

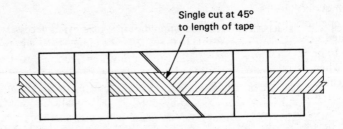

Single cut at 45°
to length of tape

Stage 2 Use a razor blade or sharp knife (or the knife incorporated in the block if there is one) to make a 45° cut across the two tapes. Remove the two waste ends, so that the cut ends butt on to each other.

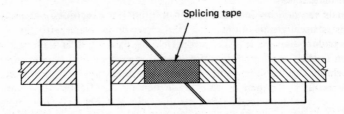

Splicing tape

Stage 3 Cut a 1 inch length of splicing tape, and place it over the join. Rub it firmly down using a fingernail or non-metallic burnisher. Trim away any excess splicing tape that extends beyond the normal width of the tape. Unclamp the tape and test the join for strength.

Figure 5.8 (continued)

Although a basic splicing block can be bought for as little as £5 or so, it may well be worth your while paying more than this (around £50-£60) for a more sophisticated block that carries out the splicing virtually automatically. If you have to carry out a lot of mechanical editing, such a device can pay for itself quickly in terms of time saved, and also produces a perfect join every time.

ELECTRONIC EDITING

Electronic editing should be carried out using two tape recorders, with the output signal of the one on which the original tape is being played being fed directly into the input of the one on which the edited tape is being recorded. Such editing should *never* be carried out by using a microphone to pick up the sound from the first machine, since this invariably causes loss of fidelity and reduction of the signal-to-noise ratio. Needless to say, the two recorders used should also be of fairly high quality. When I am carrying out such editing, I usually record from an open-reel machine on to a good cassette machine, particularly if the edited tape is to take the form of a master cassette from which copies are to be made.

When carrying out electronic editing, the output level of the first machine and the recording level of the second machine should be adjusted manually so as to produce a satisfactorily strong signal on the edited tape; the automatic recording level facility on the latter should *not* be used, since this leads to unacceptably high noise levels during silent or quiet sections (see page 128). The two machines should also be started and stopped during the dubbing process by means of their 'pause' controls, since this avoids the clicks and transient distortions that can result from the use of the 'play' and 'stop' controls.

Mixing sounds from different sources One advantage that electronic editing has over mechanical editing is that two or more separate sound signals can be simultaneously recorded on the final tape if necessary. This is usually done by feeding the separate signals into a mixer, an electronic device that enables their relative volumes to be adjusted, and then feeding the output signal from the mixer into the actual recording machine. Such a system can be used to add background music, sound effects, etc to a basic narrative.

Use of variable speed recording Another modification that can be made to recorded speech during electronic editing is alteration of the word rate. The normal speaking rate is roughly 150-200 words per minute (wpm), but research has shown that most people are capable of assimilating spoken information at a much higher rate than this without difficulty. By using a technique known as speech compression, such increases in word rate can be achieved without the rise in pitch and 'Donald Duck' distortion that result if the tape is simply speeded up. This involves passing the sound signal through special electronic circuits that remove tiny fragments from the sound at regular intervals and then join the remaining sections up to produce a shorter signal in which the words are presented at a greater rate. The process is illustrated in Figure 5.9.

By using this technique, it is possible to increase the speed of most recordings by up to 50 per cent without any appreciable loss of comprehension, although a smaller increase is probably advisable if the material is highly technical or otherwise intrinsically difficult or demanding. Clearly, use of speech compression can enable a greater amount of material to be covered in a given time or on a tape of given length. It can prove particularly useful in the preparation of material for individual listening.

A similar technique can be used to reduce the word rate of recorded speech. This involves chopping the original sound into short sections, moving these apart, and filling each gap with an extension of the previous section.

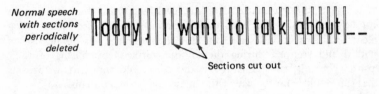

Normal speech   Today, I want to talk about __

Normal speech with sections periodically deleted

Sections cut out

Remaining sections joined up to produce compressed speech   Today, I want to talk about _____

Figure 5.9 **The technique by which speech is compressed without distortion**

PRODUCING DUPLICATES AND MULTIPLE COPIES OF TAPES

Once the final edited version of a tape has been produced, it is generally advisable to use it as a master for the production of one or more copies, preferably in cassette form. Such copies can be produced in two ways. The first involves playing the master tape on one tape recorder and feeding the signal into a second recorder — a similar process to the electronic editing described above. This method can be used if only a small number of copies is required. The second method involves making use of special high-speed copying equipment that enables several copies of the tape to be made simultaneously. Use of such equipment is obviously advisable if a large number of copies is required.

When making copies of cassette tapes for use by individual listeners it is, incidentally, often a good idea to record the material on both sides of the cassette; this saves the user from having to re-wind the tape after use — or the next user from having to re-wind the tape after someone else has failed to do so.

Many of the above aspects of audiotape recording are covered in an excellent series of leaflets written by N Nichol and published by the Scottish Council for Educational Technology (see Bibliography).

How to Design and Produce Audio Materials for Specific Purposes

Now that we have dealt with the technical aspects of audiotape recording and editing, let us end this chapter by looking at how to design audio materials for specific purposes. As we saw earlier, such materials can be used in a large number of ways in different types of instructional situations, but it is possible to divide them into four broad categories:

1. Materials used for illustrative or background purposes.
2. Materials that constitute an expository mediated lesson of some sort.
3. Materials that are designed to *manage* an instructional process of some sort.
4. Materials that provide a vehicle with which learners can interact.

Let us therefore take a look at some of the basic principles that should underlie the design of each of these categories of materials.

Illustrative and Background Materials

Materials in this category, usually intended for use in mass instructional or group-learning situations, come in a wide range of types. They can include such things as recordings of pieces of music, poems, extracts from plays and speeches — anything, in fact, that a teacher or instructor feels will enhance the quality of a particular learning experience for a particular group of people. Because of the wide-ranging nature of materials of this type, it is clearly impossible to lay down highly detailed guidelines for their design and production. As with all other types of instructional materials, the key stages are:

☐ Identification of the role that the materials are to play in the instructional situation.
☐ Planning and/or design of materials that will be best suited for carrying out this role, including the preparation of a detailed script, if necessary.
☐ Production of the actual materials.

Let us illustrate this process by considering a specific example — namely, an English teacher who wants to produce recordings of certain poems for use in a lesson on literary criticism.

STAGE 1 : IDENTIFICATION OF INSTRUCTIONAL ROLE OF MATERIALS
Let us assume that our hypothetical teacher is planning to give a lesson on (say) the different styles of a given poet at different periods in his career, or on the contrasting styles of different poets in treating similar subjects. He decides that the best way to introduce the class to the poems would be to have them recited, and feels that the impact of the verse would be much greater if the recitations were polished and 'professional'; hence the decision to pre-record them rather than to try to read or recite them 'from cold' at the actual time of the lesson.

STAGE 2 : PLANNING OF MATERIALS
Clearly, the main thing that our teacher has to do here is decide exactly which poems (or extracts from poems) would be most suitable for use in the particular situation he has in mind, and also decide on the

sequence in which they should be presented. Next, it is necessary to decide who will carry out the recitations, some of the available options being:

- To perform all the recitations himself.
- To get someone else to perform all the recitations (a colleague who has a particularly good speaking voice or a training in drama, for example).
- To get different people to recite different poems or extracts.

Whichever course of action is adopted, it is then obviously necessary to make sure that the presenter(s) is(are) thoroughly briefed and, if necessary, rehearsed so that the actual recording will run smoothly.

STAGE 3 : PRODUCING THE MATERIALS
This should be done in the way described in the previous section, the various stages being:

- ☐ Selection of appropriate equipment and materials (microphone, tape recorder and tape).
- ☐ Selection of a suitable environment in which the recording can take place and, if necessary, modification of that environment in order to improve its acoustic properties.
- ☐ Making original recordings of the various items.
- ☐ Editing these original recordings into a master tape and, if this is felt necessary, preparation of a copy of the same.

Expository Materials

This category includes all the various audio materials that present a complete lesson, lecture or instructional sequence without reference to other materials such as textbooks or notes. In other words, the material conveys the actual *content* of the lesson, lecture or sequence to the learner as well as structuring and pacing the learning process.

When designing such materials, whether for use in mass instruction, individualized instruction or group learning, the main thing to remember is that the material will be listened to, not read. Thus it is necessary to adopt a different style of writing to that which would be appropriate for (say) a set of handout notes. The style should be conversational rather than formal, avoiding the use of long, convoluted sentences and complicated phraseology, which can make spoken material virtually impossible to follow. Try to make the material easy for the listener to understand, repeating or reinforcing key points wherever possible, and making maximum use of illustrations and examples. Also never forget that the material must be completely self-contained, incorporating *all* the content that you want to get across to the listener. Needless to say this is particularly important in the case of audio materials designed for use in self-instructional situations, where there is no teacher or instructor on hand to amplify or explain what has been covered.

The planning and production of expository audio materials should be carried out in the same three stages as were described above for illustrative and background materials, namely (i) identification of their instructional role, (ii) planning and design of the materials, including (in this case) the preparation of a detailed script, and (iii) the actual production of the materials.

An example of a script prepared for a typical expository audiotape — the start of a 'tape lecture' on alternative energy — is given in Figure 5.10. This shows the sort of style that should be used when writing such material.

'In this tape, we will discuss the subject of "alternative energy". We will do so in four stages. First, we will explain exactly what is meant by the term "alternative energy", since it often means different things to different people. Second, we will look at some of the reasons why people are now taking an increasing interest in alternative energy. Third, we will take a detailed look at some of the more important forms of alternative energy that are currently being developed or appraised. In this section, we will pay particular attention to alternative methods of generating electricity — probably the most important application of alternative energy. Finally, we will try to make a realistic assessment of the contribution that alternative energy sources are likely to make to our future energy needs — both in the short term and in the long term.'

(four second pause)

'Let us now begin our examination of alternative energy by trying to establish exactly what is meant by the term. You probably have your own ideas about this already. For example, you have probably seen water mills and windmills — both of which rely on alternative forms of energy — wind energy and water energy — to produce their power. Also, you have probably seen the solar panels that many people are now fitting on their roofs in order to heat water. These, too, rely on an alternative source of energy — in this case, the sun. What, then, is the thing that distinguishes these forms of energy — and all the other so-called "alternative" sources of energy — from "conventional" energy sources? The answer is really quite simple. Basically ....'

and so on

Figure 5.10 **The start of the script of a typical tape lecture**

Management of Learning Material

In practice, this category of materials overlaps with the other categories to a considerable extent, since many audio materials whose main function is to manage or structure an instructional process also contain illustrative or background material, expository material or materials with which the learners have to interact. Such materials are mainly used in individualized instructional situations, although they are sometimes also used in group learning.

One of the most important uses of audio materials in the management of instruction is in the so-called audio-tutorial (or AT) system.

Here, an audiotape serves as the central, managerial component of a multi-media, multi-activity study unit or module, and can perform a wide range of different functions, depending on the exact nature of the unit or module. These include:

☐ Providing information of one form or another.
☐ Directing the learner to various learning activities — reading sections of textbooks, examining materials, making observations, performing experiments, completing worksheets, and so on.
☐ Providing questions to which the learner has to reply, together with feedback on the answers.
☐ Providing 'extension material' that builds upon what has been learned from the other materials and activities in the unit, eg in the form of an in-depth discussion of important points.

The planning, design and production of the audio components of instructional systems of this type must obviously be carried out within the overall context of the design of the whole system. Again, the work should be carried out in the three basic stages described in the section on expository materials: (i) identification of the instructional role (or roles) of the audio component; (ii) the planning and design of the audio materials, including the writing of a highly detailed script; and (iii) the actual production of the materials.

Specific examples of the use of audio materials in conjunction with other materials will be discussed in detail in the next chapter but, in the meantime, a specimen script is given in Figure 5.11. This is the start of an audio-tutorial on alternative energy, and should be compared with the tape-lecture script on the same subject that is given in Figure 5.10.

'In this unit of the course, we will look at the subject of "alternative energy". The objectives of the unit are listed on page one of the accompanying text. Please stop the tape and read these when you hear the signal, starting the tape again once you have finished.

(Bleep, followed by five second pause)

'As you have seen, the first objective of the unit is to enable you to explain exactly what is meant by the term "alternative energy". You probably have your own ideas about this even now, so would you please stop the tape when you hear the signal and write down, in not more than 50 words, what you think it is that distinguishes the so-called "alternative" forms of energy from the so-called "conventional" forms. Start the tape again once you have finished.'

(Bleep, followed by five second pause)

and so on

Figure 5.11 **The start of the script of a typical audio-tutorial**

Materials With Which Learners Can Interact

In this category, we include all the different audio materials that themselves provide a vehicle with which learners can interact. Probably the most important type are the various materials that are used as software in language laboratories and similar audio-electronic classrooms, so we shall concentrate on these in this section.

THE DIFFERENT TYPES OF LANGUAGE LABORATORY

Before discussing the design and preparation of language laboratory materials, it would probably be useful to explain exactly what a language laboratory is and describe the main types that are currently in use. Essentially a language laboratory is a facility that enables individual learners (working either alone or as part of a class or group) to listen to and respond to spoken material of various forms through the medium of a headset linked to a central or individual tape recorder. Three types of laboratory are in common use.

Audio-Active Comparative (AAC) Laboratories These are full-scale class systems containing up to 30 individual carrels, each linked to a master console operated by the teacher or instructor in charge of the laboratory (see Figure 5.12). Each carrel has its own tape recorder, as has the master console, from which all the individual carrels can be monitored or controlled, either singly or in groups. Such laboratories enable individual learners to work at their own pace, to rewind their own tapes and repeat sections if necessary, and — most important — to record and listen to their own responses (hence the word 'comparative' in the name).

Figure 5.12 **A typical audio-active comparative language laboratory**

Audio-Active (AA) Laboratories These are again full-class systems comprising individual carrels linked to a master console, but differ from AAC laboratories in that the carrels are not equipped with their own tape recorders. Instead, the students receive their material from the master console. In such systems, the students can listen to and respond to material and can also hear their responses via their microphone and headphones; they cannot record their responses, however, and also have to work in lockstep at a pace controlled by the person operating the master console. Audio-active laboratories are cheaper to install and operate than audio-active comparative laboratories, and appear to be almost as effective for most purposes.

Mini-Laboratories A mini-laboratory consists of a single study unit, usually audio-active comparative and portable. Such units can be used independently, for individual instruction, or can be linked with similar units to form a full-scale AAC laboratory controlled from a suitable master console. Flexible systems of this type are now becoming increasingly widely used.

PRODUCING SOFTWARE FOR LANGUAGE LABORATORIES
The design and preparation of software for use in language laboratories is a highly specialized business and, in a general book of this nature, it is not possible to do any more than offer a few general guidelines.

First, it is important not to regard a language laboratory merely as a tool for polishing pronunciation, practising grammar and similar routine and uninspiring activities. When properly used, such laboratories can provide learners with an interesting and highly motivating means of improving their oral and aural performance, extending their vocabulary, and reinforcing general principles learned in open class. By individualizing the learning process, they also tend to improve concentration and, of course, provide each learner with greater opportunities for personal language practice than would be possible in a conventional classroom. In too many cases, however, the use of poorly designed software and excessive use of 'drill and practice' at the expense of more interesting and demanding activities lead to student boredom and failure to get the most out of the system. Thus it is vital that all language laboratory software should be carefully planned and designed, taking full account of the role that it is intended to play in the instructional process. Some of the basic activities that can be built into such software are given below.

☐ Pronunciation practice, in which the student is provided with a series of spoken exemplars which he has to try to imitate. Some sort of four-phase pattern is probably best (exemplar, student imitation, repeat of exemplar, repeat of imitation).

☐ Structured pattern drills, in which the student is presented with a standard pattern (eg *il a mangé une orange*) and then has to repeat it with different subjects (*elle, nous, vous*, etc) or objects, use the same structure with different verbs, and so on.

☐ Sentence-building exercises, in which the learner is presented with different pieces of information or phrases that have to be structured into complete sentences.

☐ Questions and answers, ranging from simple questions in a highly structured situation where the answer is fairly obvious to more open-ended questions where a variety of answers are possible (proper structuring of the debriefing section is vital here).

☐ Aural comprehension, eg giving the learners some questions in advance, with the answers being contained in a taped passage that they then have to listen to; letting them listen to a taped passage first and then asking questions; making them summarize a passage to which they have listened; and so on.

☐ Role-playing exercises, eg exercises in which the learner first has to listen to a section of dialogue (preferably twice), this then being replayed with one of the roles missing so that the learner can participate.

☐ Games, eg quizzes based on true/false responses or multiple-choice answers, or guessing games in which the learner is given a series of clues and then has to supply the answer.

☐ Specific linguistic activities, eg asking the learner to persuade someone to do something, explain something, complain about something, and so on.

☐ Changing passages from direct to indirect speech.

No doubt readers can think of many other ways in which language laboratories and similar facilities can be used.

When it comes to the actual production of materials for language laboratories, one of the most important things to remember is that the *pauses* are just as important as the *spoken content*, both in terms of their position and in terms of their length. It is probably best to start by recording all the spoken material, without pauses, and then to edit this material on to a master tape, incorporating the pauses as you do so. This will enable you to concentrate on one thing at a time.

In the case of an audio-active laboratory, it is normally only necessary to prepare a single copy of the master tape. In the case of an audio-active comparative laboratory, on the other hand, there will be many occasions when it is necessary to provide the students with their own copies of the recorded material. This can either be done in advance, by preparing multiple copies from the master tape, or can be done at the time of the lesson, by playing the relevant section(s) of the master tape at the master console and having the students record the material on their individual machines.

Bibliography

Anderson, R H (1976) *Selection and Developing Media for Instruction.* Van Nostrand Reinhold, Cincinnati (Chapter 7).

Hill, B (1976) *Teaching Aids and Resources*. In *Teaching Languages*, British Broadcasting Corporation, London.

Jones, J G (1972) *Teaching With Tape*. Focal Press, London and New York.

Kemp, J E (1980) *Planning and Producing Audiovisual Materials*. Harper and Row, New York (Chapter 17).

Nichol, N *SCET Guidelines on Audiorecording* (a series of leaflets). Scottish Council for Educational Technology, Glasgow.

Postlethwaite, S N, Novak, J and Murray, H (1972) *The Audio-Tutorial Approach to Learning*. Burgess, Minneapolis.

Romiszowski, A J (1974) *The Selection and Use of Instructional Media*. Kogan Page, London (Chapter 6).

Wittich, W A and Schuller, C F (1979) *Instructional Technology — Its Nature and Use*. Harper and Row, New York (Chapter 6).

Chapter 6
How to Produce Linked Audio and Still Visual Materials

Introduction

In Chapters 2 to 4, we examined the three basic classes of still visual display materials, looking first at printed and duplicated materials, then at non-projected materials and finally at projected materials, while in Chapter 5, we discussed simple audio materials. In this chapter, we will turn our attention to the various hybrid systems that use audio materials in conjunction with these different types of still visual materials, thus enabling multi-sensory stimulation of the learner to take place.

As in previous chapters, we·will begin by examining the various ways in which linked audio and still visual materials can be used in mass instruction, individualized learning and group learning — the three basic types of instructional situation that were identified in Chapter 1. Then, we will examine some of the most important types of system, looking first at systems that link audiotapes with textual materials, then at systems that link tape with series of slides or photographic prints, and finally at various other combinations such as 'tape-model', 'tape-microscope' and 'tape-realia'. In each case, we will identify the main uses of the system and then show how the materials can be designed and produced.

How Linked Audio and Still Visual Materials can be Used in Different Teaching/Learning Situations

Like all the other types of materials discussed so far, linked audio and still visual materials can be used in a wide range of instructional situations. Let us now see what roles they are capable of playing in each of the three basic classes we have divided such situations into.

Mass Instruction

As I see it, linked audio and still visual materials have two main roles in mass instruction. First, they can be used to provide background and illustrative material within the context of a conventional 'live' expository lesson, media such as tape-slide programmes and filmstrips-with-sound being ideal for these purposes. Second, they can be used to provide mediated presentations to a class, tape-slide programmes and filmstrips-with-sound again being ideal media for this, together with radio-vision programmes. In both cases, the use of such media can introduce welcome variety into a course.

Individualized Instruction

Until the advent of computer-based learning, the various systems that use audio and still visual materials in combination were probably the most effective tool available to anyone designing an individualized instruction course of practically any type. Indeed, there are a large number of cases where such systems are still the best medium for individualized instruction, as we will see later in this chapter. Systems such as tape-slide and filmstrips-with-sound have long been used in this role, and the great potential of other linked audio and still visual media such as 'tape-text', 'tape-model', 'tape-microscope' and 'tape-realia' is only now beginning to be fully realized.

Group Learning

Here, the main role of linked audio and still visual materials is probably the provision of illustrative and background material, although there is also scope for the use of such materials as a vehicle for small-group activities. Media such as 'tape-model' and 'tape-realia' certainly have potential here.

LINKED TAPE AND TEXTUAL MATERIALS

As we saw in the last chapter, audiotapes linked with textual materials in an integrated audio-tutorial system constitute a useful vehicle for individualized instruction (see page 136). Here, the tape forms the central 'managerial' component of the instructional system, providing the learner with information, directing him to various activities (reading passages from books or notes, examining materials, carrying out exercises, etc) and providing aural back-up to and extension of these activities. Such systems can be used in the teaching of virtually any subject, and have the great advantage of getting the learner actively involved rather than simply being a passive receiver of information.

Another way of using tape in conjunction with text is to link it directly with a specific worksheet or workbook, so that the two media — audio and textual — are fully integrated. In such systems, the role of the tape may be to introduce the topic to be covered, explain and/or describe the content, periodically direct the learner to activities in the worksheet or workbook, and provide aural back-up and extension material related to these activities. The main role of the worksheet or workbook will probably be to provide questions, exercises, problems, etc, although it may also be used to give the student a permanent 'personal copy' of the material covered by the system, provide self-assessment tests, provide 'further reading' lists, and so on.

How to Plan and Design Tape-Text Materials

When planning tape-text materials — or, indeed, any materials that make use of more than one sense or medium — the primary aim should be to produce a fully integrated instructional system that makes optimum use of the different media being employed. Thus, each of the media should be used in a role that takes full advantage of its particular characteristics and, most importantly, the different components should *complement* one another. When planning such a system, you will probably find it useful to go through the following stages:

☐ Establish a clear set of instructional objectives for the system, preferably couched in behavioural terms.

☐ Taking full account of the relevant circumstances (target population, overall role of materials, etc), decide on the basic content of the whole system.

☐ Decide what activities would be appropriate for covering this content and overtaking the instructional objectives, and establish the role of the different media in each activity. Prepare an outline description of the whole system, clearly defining these activities and roles.

☐ Write the various textual components of the system, always bearing in mind the role that the accompanying audiotape is going to play when they are being used.

☐ Produce a detailed script for the audiotape, including pauses and recording instructions.

☐ Record the spoken material for the tape without pauses, preferably using an open-reel machine (see page 126).

☐ Dub the spoken material on to a master tape (either open-reel or cassette), editing in the pauses and any other sound(s) required as you do so (see page 130).

☐ Produce as many copies of the tape as are required by copying the master tape on to one or more compact cassettes, preferably recording the material on both sides of the cassette (see page 132).

☐ Produce copies of the textual materials after making any changes found necessary in the course of producing the tape.

An example of a script for the audiotape component of an audio-tutorial (on alternative energy) was given in Figure 5.11, and a further example of tape-text material is given in Figure 6.1. This is the start of the outline description that I recently prepared when planning an audio-workbook on writing instructional objectives.

Writing Instructional Objectives – An Audio-Workbook	
Audiotape	*Workbook*
	Title; instructions to start tape
Introduction to audio-workbook, stating overall aims and outlining content (roughly two minutes). Instructions to study detailed objectives in workbook and to re-start tape when finished. (Bleep, followed by five second pause).	
	Full statement of instructional objectives of audio-workbook expressed in behavioural terms.
Recapitulation of first objective, relating to the role of objectives in a systematic approach to course or curriculum design; referral to schematic diagram of such an approach in workbook. (roughly three minutes). Instructions to summarize three key functions of objectives just described in spaces provided in workbook, rewinding tape and replaying section if necessary, and to re-start tape when finished. (Bleep, followed by five second pause).	Block diagram showing role of objectives in course or curriculum design process.
	Labelled spaces for writing in three key function of objectives.
Recapitulation of second objective, relating to the distinction between *aims* and *objectives*. Instructions to study examples given in workbook and to re-start tape when finished. (Bleep, followed by five second pause).	
	Example of a typical aim (from the section of a secondary school chemistry course dealing with chemical bonding) followed by the start of the list of detailed objectives associated with that aim.

Figure 6.1 **The start of the outline of a typical audio-workbook**

Audiotape	Workbook
Discussion of the distinction between aims and objectives, with reference to the illustrative material in the text (roughly two minutes). Instructions to summarize distinctions between aims and objectives in spaces provided in workbook, rewinding tape and replaying section if necessary, and to re-start tape when finished. (Bleep, followed by five second pause).	
	Labelled spaces for writing in distinguishing features of aims and objectives.
Recapitulation of third objective . . . and so on	

Figure 6.1 (continued)

The way in which the audio and textual components of an audio-workbook can be used to support and complement one another is clearly illustrated in this example.

Linked Tape and Photographic Materials

The various systems that link audiotapes with sequences of photographic images are among the most widely used of all audiovisual media — particularly as vehicles for individualized instruction. Of the various types of system, the two that can most easily be produced 'in-house' by practising teachers, instructors and trainers are tape-slide programmes and tape-photograph programmes, so we will concentrate on these in this section.

Tape-Slide Programmes

Tape-slide programmes consist of linked sequences of photographic slides, usually of the compact 2 inch x 2 inch variety, that are accompanied by synchronized commentaries recorded on audiotape, usually on compact cassettes. In some cases, synchronization of the advance of the slides with the sound is achieved by incorporating audible 'bleeps' in the actual sound signal, so that the user knows when to advance the slides manually. In more sophisticated programmes designed for display on fully automatic equipment, the advance cues are recorded on a separate track of the tape, consisting of pulses of sound that trigger the 'advance' mechanism on the slide projection or viewing system. Both forms of programme can be used in virtually all types of instructional situation by using appropriate equipment. For showing a tape-slide programme to a class or large group, this usually consists of a slide projector and separate audiotape player, with the two being linked by an electronic synchronizing unit if the programme is an 'automatic' one with inaudible advance cues. For individual or small-group use, the equipment can range from a simple manual slide viewer and cheap cassette player to a fully automatic tape-slide unit incorporating linked audio playback and back-projection slide viewing facilities.

INSTRUCTIONAL USES OF TAPE-SLIDE PROGRAMMES

As we have seen, tape-slide programmes can be used in virtually all types of instructional situation, both as self-contained units of mediated instruction and also in a secondary or supportive role (providing illustrative material, background material, and so on). When used in the former role, such programmes can be just as effective as a well-prepared, well-delivered lecture or expository lesson in helping students to understand the subject matter. Like the latter, however, they constitute an essentially 'one-way' channel of communication in which the learner has no opportunity for active participation, so that long-term retention of the material tends to be low. Thus it is now generally agreed that tape-slide programmes are most useful as a vehicle for giving a general introduction to a topic, or of stimulating interest and providing motivation for further or more detailed study, rather than as a vehicle for presenting the detailed content of a course. To teach this detailed content effectively, it is advisable to use methods that incorporate higher learner involvement. A more detailed discussion of the strengths and weaknesses of tape-slide programmes as instructional vehicles is given in the book by Romiszowski listed in the Bibliography, and interested readers are referred to this.

HOW TO DESIGN AND PRODUCE TAPE-SLIDE PROGRAMMES

General guidelines: When designing a tape-slide programme for a specific educational or training purpose, it is obviously necessary to be quite clear what this purpose is, and to be satisfied that use of a tape-slide programme is likely to be an effective way of achieving it. Assuming that this is the case, I would offer readers the following general guidelines.

☐ Keep the programme simple. As we have seen, the tape-slide medium is best suited to providing general introductions to topics rather than to providing detailed coverage of their content.

☐ Keep the programme comparatively short — certainly no longer than the 80 slides that can be contained in the standard carousel-type magazines that are used with most automatic tape-slide equipment.

☐ Make sure that the programme has a clearly defined structure, making appropriate use of 'signposts' and 'links' to ensure that the user has no difficulty in seeing what this structure is.

☐ Make sure that the visual and audio elements complement each other at all times (this is probably the most important rule of all).

☐ Do not compromise on quality; a tape-slide programme is only as good as its weakest component, so try to make sure that the photographs, the graphic slides, the narration, and (most important of all) the synchronization are all of the same equally high standard.

The detailed design of the programme: This is best carried out by first producing a skeleton outline, listing the main sections of the programme, and then writing a detailed script for the programme — either in the form of a 'story board' (sketches of the individual frames with the accompanying text alongside) or as a double-column script with the visual component described on one side and the audio element on the other.

Whichever form of script you decide to employ, you should try to make full and effective use of the different types of basic 'building bricks' that can be used to construct tape-slide programmes. I find it helpful to classify these as follows:

Visual 'building bricks'

☐ Signposts and links (main title slides, titles for sections and sub-sections, and so on).

☐ Photographs (original or 'second-hand' photographic images of all types).

☐ Graphic illustrations (schematic diagrams, graphs, bar charts, pie charts, tables, and so on).

☐ Verbal illustrations (slides carrying simple verbal material designed to support or complement the narrative).

Audio 'building bricks'

☐ Narrative (the main component of the audio element of all tape-slide programmes).

☐ Silence (the pauses between frames, and any other deliberate pauses or periods of silence).

☐ Music (introductory or closing music, music used as a link between sections, background music, and so on).

☐ Special effects (claps of thunder, shots, sounds of machinery, or any other special sound effects thought appropriate at specific points in a programme).

I find that I always use the first six, but only use the last two on very rare occasions. In the case of music, this is partly because there are generally copyright problems associated with the use of music on tape-slide programmes, and partly because I find the use of music in such programmes (other than in introductory, linking and closing sequences) distracting.

SEDCO Non-Destructive Testing Appreciation Course
Stage 1: Basic Concepts and Techniques

Slide sequence and commentary for tape-slide programme

Slides	*Commentary* (pulses signified by *)
1. Main title slide: 'SEDCO Non-Destructive Testing Appreciation Course' Stage 1: basic concepts and techniques	*Silence* (ten seconds) followed by *
2. Photograph of SEDCO personnel (with SEDCO logo clearly visible on helmets) inspecting the flange on the end of a section of pipeline in their pipe yard prior to carrying out a test for cracks.	'The programme that you are about to see has been specially produced for SEDCO in order to give you and your colleagues an introduction to the field of *non-destructive testing*, or *NDT* as it is commonly called.' *(one second pause; * ; one second pause)*
3. Photograph of front cover of self-instructional manual that accompanies programme, showing name of Company.	'You should also have received a copy of the SEDCO self-tuition manual that has been written to accompany the programme, and should read this carefully after you have finished studying the programme itself.' *(one second pause; * ; one second pause)*
4. Caption slide listing first set of self-assessment questions in manual.	'At the end of each section of the manual, you will find a number of questions dealing with the material covered. These have been designed to help you tell whether you have mastered the material, or whether you will need to go over some of it again.' *(four second pause; * ; one second pause)*
5. Photograph of SEDCO personnel carrying out MPI test on flange on pipeline.	'Once you are satisfied that you can answer *all* the questions in the manual, you will be ready to move on to Stage 2 of the course, which examines some of the ways in which non-destructive testing is actually used by SEDCO.' *(one second pause; *)*
6. Section title slide: 'NDT as a diagnostic tool'	*Silence* (ten seconds) followed by *

Figure 6.2 **The start of the script of a typical instructional tape-slide programme**

Slides	*Commentary* (pulses signified by *)
7. Caption slide 'NDT — examining materials for flaws without impairing their desirable properties'.	'Non-destructive testing has been defined as the science of examining materials or manufactured articles in order to determine their fitness for a certain purpose, *without impairing their desirable properties in any way*.' (*one second pause;* * ; *one second pause*)
8. Schematic diagram, showing two possible outcomes of NDT: (1) no serious defects ∴ OK for use. (2) serious defects ∴ unsuitable for use.	'No material or manufactured article is ever *completely* free from flaws or defects, and the object of NDT is to detect any such defects and determine whether they are likely to be sufficiently serious to prevent the item from being able to do the job for which it was designed.' (*three second pause;* * ; *one second pause*)
9. Schematic diagram of block of material showing surface and internal defects.	'Defects are of two basic types, namely, those that occur on the surface of an item, and those that are located in the interior, and are thus much more difficult to detect.' (*one second pause;* * ; *one second pause*)
10. Caption slide listing three types of NDT tests: — surface tests — sub-surface tests — internal tests.	'We find it convenient to divide non-destructive testing methods into three broad groups, depending on the type of defects that they are designed to detect, namely, *surface tests;* which are used to detect defects that occur on the actual surface; *sub-surface tests,* which are able to detect defects that are located just below the surface; and *internal tests*, which can be used to discover defects that occur deep in the interior.' (*one second pause;* * ; *one second pause*)
11. Caption slide listing two main types of NDT methods to be covered in programme: — dye penetrant testing — magnetic particle inspection.	'A large number of different NDT techniques are available, but the ones that you are most likely to make use of in the course of your work are *dye penetrant testing* and *magnetic particle inspection.* We will therefore take a detailed look at each of these methods.' (*one second pause;* * ; *one second pause*)

Figure 6.2 (continued)

Slides	Commentary (pulses signified by ∗)
12. Caption slide listing other four types of NDT methods to be covered: — eddy current testing — ultrasonic testing — X-ray radiography — gamma radiography.	'We will also examine four other important NDT methods with which you should be familiar, even though you are unlikely to have to use them yourself — eddy current testing, ultrasonic testing, X-ray radiography and gamma radiography.' (one second pause; ∗)
13. Section title slide: 'Dye penetrant testing'.	Silence (ten seconds) followed by ∗.
and so on	

Figure 6.2 (continued)

Part of a typical script for a tape-slide programme is given in Figure 6.2. This was written for the South-Eastern Drilling Company (SEDCO) as part of a distance learning package on non-destructive testing that my colleague, Eric Addinall, and I developed for the Company in 1982.

The 75-slide programme from which the script extract is presented was used to provide a general introduction to the subject of non-destructive testing, being accompanied by a 68-page self-instructional manual that dealt with the subject in much greater detail. The development of the package is described in detail in the paper by Ellington, Addinall and Blood that is listed in the Bibliography.

Figure 6.2 illustrates many of the basic principles of tape-slide programme design, and readers should note the following specific points:

☐ The clear division of the programme into sections using title slides and periods of silence; the latter can, alternatively, be filled with suitable music if this is preferred.

☐ The explicit specification of the lengths of the pauses between slides and the timing of the slide changes. These are crucial to the success of a programme, which can easily be ruined if the pauses are too short (or too long), or if the slide changes are badly timed.

☐ The way in which the visual elements have been carefully designed to complement the narrative which, in this particular programme, is the main vehicle of communication. Wherever possible, a photograph or schematic diagram is used but, in cases where neither of these would be appropriate, a simple caption slide that reinforces the key points being made in the narrative is employed (see, for example, frames 7, 10, 11 and 12). The later sections of the programme, which deal with the various NDT methods, make use of a similar mixture of photographs, schematic diagrams and 'verbal reinforcement' slides to back up the narrative.

☐ The way in which the various visual elements are explicitly described in the script — the verbal equivalent of the sketches in a 'story board' script.

Producing the programme materials: The two processes described above — producing the skeleton outline and producing the detailed script — constitute the first two stages in the development of a tape-slide programme. As can be seen from Figure 6.3, which shows the complete development process in a flow diagram form, the next stage consists of the actual production of the audio and visual components of the programme — two processes that should be carried out in parallel.

The audio side of the work involves three separate processes:

☐ Recording the commentary for the programme in the way described on pages 126 to 128 of Chapter 5. I generally engage the services of a professional presenter for this work, particularly if the programme is an important one, but appreciate that this may not always be practicable; if not, make sure that the presenter used is capable of doing justice to the material (see page 126).

☐ Recording or acquiring any other sound components needed for the programme (music, sound effects, etc). If you do decide to make use of music, make sure that you have proper copyright clearance, otherwise you could find yourself in severe legal difficulties; by far the safest way to proceed is to have your own music specially composed and performed.

☐ Dubbing the commentary and any other sound components on to a master cassette tape, in the way described on pages 130 to 131 of Chapter 5, editing in the pauses and periods of silence as you do so. The easiest way to time such pauses is to 'count in thousands' ('one thousand', 'two thousand', 'three thousand', and so on) which, with a little practice, can be used to time multiples of one second with considerable accuracy. Do not edit in the pulses at this stage, since this is best deferred until you have the complete set of slides available.

The visual side of the work involves five separate processes:

☐ Designing all the various graphic slides (main title slides, section title slides, schematic diagrams, graphs, caption slides, etc). I find that this is best done by producing a rough version of the material required on each slide on a separate sheet of paper, using coloured felt pens.

☐ Producing the finished artwork for the graphic slides. If you have to do this yourself, use the various techniques described on pages 73 to 75 of Chapter 3 but, if at all possible, it is obviously better to have the work done by a specialist graphic artist.

☐ Producing the graphic slides, in the way described on pages 108 to 111 of Chapter 4.

☐ Producing the photographic slides (ie those slides that consist of original photographs rather than photographs of artwork). This should be done in the way described on pages 105 to 108 of Chapter 4.

☐ Assembling the master set of slides. I use one of the display racks in my slide storage/display cabinet for this work (see Figure 4.11), after which I transfer the complete set into a carousel-type magazine or transfer storage box. This has the advantage of visually displaying the complete sequence of slides during the assembly process.

Once you have produced the edited master tape and assembled the full slide sequence for the programme, the crucial task of pulsing the master tape can be carried out. This can either be done using a suitable cassette tape recorder that possesses a pulsing facility or using an individual tape-slide playback/viewing machine that possesses a similar facility. Whichever method is used, check that the pulses will operate the equipment that you will be using to show the tape-slide programme, since pulses recorded on one type of equipment do not always work with another.

Finally, run off as many using copies of the programme as are required by producing duplicate copies of the master cassette in the way described on page 132 of Chapter 5 and producing duplicates of the slides in the way described on page 113 of Chapter 4.

Storing tape-slide programmes: One problem that has to be overcome by all users of tape-slide programmes is that of storing the programme materials — especially the slides. If the programme is short, it is possible simply to store the slides in a small box, eg an empty slide binder box, and to load them into the viewing or projection equipment one by one at the time of use. With longer programmes, however, this becomes very time-consuming, and it is much better to store the complete slide sequence in such a way that it is immediately ready for use. If the equipment that is to be used to show or view the programme employs a carousel-type magazine, the slides can either be stored in an actual magazine or else in a slide transfer storage box — a circular box that enables an entire programme to be transferred to or from the projector magazine simply by placing one on top of the other and then upending the system.

Tape-Photograph Programmes

A tape-photograph programme is simply a linked sequence of photographic prints with an accompanying audio-tape. Such programmes can be used to do virtually anything that a conventional tape-slide programme can do, and have two advantages over the latter. First, they require no projection or viewing equipment, since photographic prints, unlike slides, are completely 'free standing'. Second, they are in some ways much more flexible and versatile than tape-slide programmes from an instructional point of view. It is, for example, much easier to incorporate textual materials into a tape-photograph programme, and also to build in enactive components such as exercises

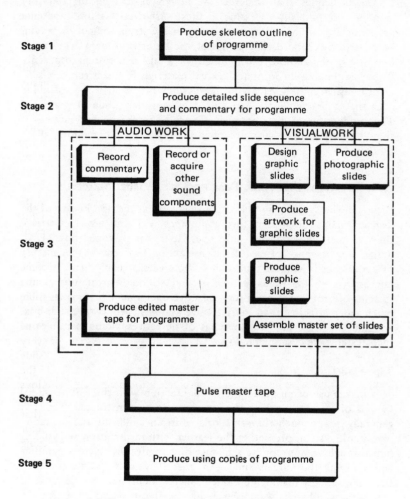

Figure 6.3 **The various stages in the design and production of a tape-slide programme**

or worksheets. Indeed an effective way of presenting the photographic component of tape-photograph programmes is to incorporate them into a re-usable workbook.

The principles that underlie the design of tape-photograph programmes are basically the same as those just described for tape-slide programmes, the main difference being in the structuring of the audio-tape narrative. Indeed, the design of the latter is in many ways more like that of the audiotape component of a tape-text system (especially if the programme incorporates textual materials or enactive exercises), incorporating audible cues and instructions rather than the inaudible cues that characterize the tapes used in most tape-slide programmes. The production of the materials for tape-photograph programmes is similar to the process just described for tape-slide programmes, albeit simpler.

Other Systems that Link Tape and Still Visual Materials

Although the systems described above are by far the best known of the instructional systems that link audiotapes with still visual materials, they are certainly not the only ones. It is, for example, possible to design a wide range of useful self-instructional systems that make use of audiotapes in conjunction with tools, pieces of equipment, models, microscope slides, items of realia, and so on. Furthermore, such systems often incorporate a high enactive component that makes them much more effective than more passive systems such as tape-slide programmes in achieving certain types of objectives. Some examples of such systems are described below.

Tape-Model

This makes use of an audiotape in conjunction with three-dimensional models or kits from which such models can be constructed. The tape generally plays much the same role as in an audio-tutorial or audio-workbook system, presenting the learner with information and guiding him through an appropriate sequence of activities that involve handling and studying the models and, in the case of systems that use construction kits, actually making up models. Such systems have a wide range of applications, obvious examples being in the teaching of chemistry (work with models of electronic orbital systems, molecules, complexes, crystal structures, and so on), biology (work with models of parts of animals and plants, physiological systems, and so on), physics (work with models of physical systems of various sorts) and engineering (work with models of machines, systems, plant and so on). Figure 6.4 shows a typical tape-model system in use (a student of chemistry using a 'ball and spring' kit to construct and study models of different organic molecules — isomers of simple alkanes, in this case).

Figure 6.4 A student of chemistry studying the isomers of the
simple alkanes using a tape-model system

Tape-Microscope

When using a microscope, it is obviously difficult to read textual
material (instructions, explanatory notes, etc) at the same time. Thus
there is obvious scope for the use of audiotapes to supply such information, since this enables the learner to work at the same time as he is
receiving the information. Subjects that lend themselves to the use of
this technique include all the various branches of biology and medicine,
geology and metallurgy.

Tape-Realia

Audiotapes can also be used to provide instructions and information to
learners who are studying realia of various forms — eg geological or
biological specimens. As in the case of tape-microscopes, use of an
audiotape to provide such information can allow complicated enactive
processes to be carried out without the distraction of having to refer to
textual instructions or notes — obviously a great advantage in an individualized learning situation.

No doubt readers can think of many other instructional situations in which audiotapes could usefully be linked with still visual materials of various types.

Designing and Producing the Courseware for Such Systems

The design of the courseware for a system that links an audiotape with the use of materials such as models or realia is basically the same as for an audio-tutorial system (see page 135), except that no textual materials are generally involved. A typical example of the script for such a system is given in Figure 6.5. This is for a self-instructional revision system in basic petrology (the branch of geology that involves the study of rocks), being designed to help students prepare for a practical examination that involves identifying hand specimens of different rocks and describing their compositions as revealed by microscopic study of thin sections cut from them.

Basic Petrology — Revision Unit: Igneous Rocks	
Contents of audiotape	*Associated activities*
This Unit is designed to help you to recognize hand specimens of the main types of igneous rocks, and to describe their mineralogical compositions as revealed by the study of thin sections of the rocks using a geological microscope. If you require any help with the use of the latter, study the accompanying instruction sheet. We will begin by studying the main types of acid plutonic rocks, ie the *granites*. Please pick up and examine Specimen 1 in the tray of hand specimens when you hear the signal, stopping the tape when you do so. Make a note of what you think are the main characteristics of this specimen, restarting the tape once you have finished. (Bleep, followed by five second pause)	Instruction sheet on geological microscope available if required.
	Study of Specimen 1 (normal granite) and noting down of observed characteristics.

Figure 6.5 **Start of the script of a typical instructional system that uses an audiotape in conjunction with enactive activities (study of geological specimens)**

Contents of audiotape	Associated activities
This is a specimen of normal granite from the Rubislaw Quarry in Aberdeen, its main constituents being quartz (the clear, colourless mineral), feldspar (the grey material) and mica (the black and clear platy materials). Note the relatively coarse texture (indicating the plutonic origins of the rock) and uniform grain size.	Re-examination of Specimen 1 as commentary proceeds.
Now let us take a look at a section of this rock using the geological microscope. Select Slide 1 from the box of slides provided and carry out a thorough examination of it, making a note of all the minerals that you identify in order of relative abundance. Stop the tape when you hear the signal, and re-start it once you have finished the work. (Bleep, followed by five second pause)	
	Study of Slide 1 using geological microscope.
As you should have seen, the predominant mineral in this particular type of granite is *quartz*. This is colourless, free from alteration, shows fluid inclusion, has a low refractive index (close to that of Canada Balsam) and shows low double refraction. Stop the tape until you are satisfied that you can recognize all these features. (Bleep, followed by five second pause)	Re-examination of slide as commentary proceeds.
	Re-examination of slide in order to identify the various features of quartz.
Next in relative abundance are various forms of *feldspar*. Of these, the most important is *orthoclase*, recognizable by its alteration, low refractive index, and low double refraction; some crystals also show Carlsbad twinning. Stop the tape until you are satisfied	Re-examination of slide as commentary proceeds.
and so on	

Figure 6.5 (continued)

The courseware should be produced in the same way as for tape-text materials (see page 143).

Bibliography

Anderson, R H (1976) *Selecting and Developing Media for Instruction*. Van Nostrand Reinhold, Cincinnati (Chapter 7).

Beaumont-Craggs, R (1975) *Slide-Tape and Dual Projection*. Focal Press, London and New York.

Ellington, H I, Addinall, E and Blood, J (1984) Providing extension training for offshore personnel — an educational technology-based approach. In Shaw, K E (ed) (1983) *Aspects of Educational Technology XVII*, Kogan Page, London, pp 168-73.

Johnstone, A H, Letton, K M and Percival, F (1977) Tape-model: the lecture complement. *Chemistry in Britain*, 13, 11, pp 423-5.

Kemp, J E (1980) *Planning and Producing Audiovisual Materials*. Harper and Row, New York (Chapter 19).

Langdon, D G (1978) The Audio Workbook. In *The Instructional Design Library* (Vol 3). Educational Technology Press, Englewood Cliffs, NJ.

Postlethwaite, S N, Novak, J and Murray, H (1978) *The Audio-Tutorial Approach to Learning*. Burgess, Minneapolis.

Romiszowski, A J (1974) *The Selection and Use of Instructional Media*. Kogan Page, London (Chapter 6).

Russell, J D (1978) The Audio-Tutorial System. In *The Instructional Design Library* (Vol 3). Educational Technology Press, Englewood Cliffs, NJ.

Chapter 7

How to Produce Cine and Video Materials

Introduction

In this chapter we will turn our attention to the two basic media that enable moving visual material to be displayed or viewed, either on their own or in conjunction with audio material — cine and video. Both media have had a considerable impact on instructional methodology with video, in particular, showing every sign of becoming even more important if the price of the associated equipment continues to fall in real terms.

As in previous chapters, we will start by taking a general look at how cine and video can be used in different types of teaching/learning situation. We will then examine the basic techniques that are involved in cine photography and editing and in video recording and editing. Finally we will discuss the planning and production of cine and video materials.

How Cine and Video Materials can be Used in Different Teaching/Learning Situations

It is probably true to say that cine and video materials can be used in virtually any type of instructional situation, either to provide illustrative or supportive material or as the vehicle by which an exposition or instructional sequence is presented. Their use is not limited — as is sometimes erroneously supposed — to situations where it is necessary to show movement, since the two media can be used for presenting visual material of all types (although they are, of course, best suited to demonstrating motion of various sorts). Let us now see how they can be used in the three broad classes of instructional situation that were identified earlier in the book — mass instruction, individualized instruction and group learning.

Mass Instruction

Here, cine and video materials have three main roles. First, they can be used to provide illustrative, background and other supportive material for use within the context of conventional expository instruction. Both media are ideally suited for this purpose and are, of course, particularly useful in situations where motion has to be demonstrated. Such 'moving visual inserts' can range from full-length films or television programmes lasting for half an hour or more to short clips or single-concept sequences lasting only a few tenths of seconds.

Second, cine and video materials can be used to provide self-contained mediated expositions that take the place of a conventional lecture or taught lesson on a given topic. When employed in this way, the two media are not necessarily restricted to showing scenes that incorporate movement, but can be used to present any material that has a strong visual component. Sequences of still pictures, for example, can often be shown just as effectively within the context of a cine or video presentation as in a tape-slide programme. All types of cine and video materials can be used in this 'mediated lesson' role, including externally produced cine films, broadcast television programmes (either off-air or recorded) and 'home-produced' cine and video presentations designed for specific purposes.

Third, cine and video materials – and especially the latter – can be used as vehicles with which learners can interact in the context of a mass instructional situation. The use of a closed-circuit television system to record drama, role-playing exercises, debates, etc for subsequent discussion and analysis by a class are typical examples.

Individualized Instruction

Being essentially a mass communication medium, cine is not the best vehicle for use in mediated individualized learning, although short single-concept loop films can sometimes form a useful component of individualized learning programmes. Cine materials can, however, easily be converted into video form, thus making them more suitable for individual use, and can also be incorporated into tape-film programmes designed for individual study. Video materials are, of course, ideally suited for use in individualized learning situations, either on their own or within the context of an interactive video system (these will be discussed in the next chapter). When used on their own, such materials are probably best suited to a straightforward expository role although the advent of interactive video should enable them to be built into a much wider range of instructional situations than has previously been possible.

Group Learning

Here, there are two main ways in which cine and video materials can be used: in a supportive role (providing visual material for illustrative, background information or extension purposes) and as a vehicle with or through which the participants have to interact (eg in role-play, simulations and micro-teaching). The video medium has already proved to be ideal for the latter role, and early evidence suggests that interactive video may prove to be even more useful in many situations.

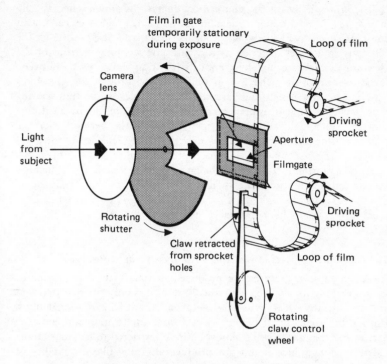

Figure 7.1 **The intermittent exposure process
by which a cine camera operates**

The Basic Principles of Cine Photography and Printing

How Cine Cameras and Projectors Operate

Motion pictures and television both create an illusion of movement by presenting the eye with a rapid sequence of still images, each slightly different from the previous one. Because of the phenomenon of persistence of vision (whereby the retina of the eye retains a particular image for some time after the stimulus that produces it is withdrawn), the human brain interprets such a sequence of images as a continuously changing system (similar to that which it is used to 'seeing' in the real world) provided that the images are presented at a rate greater than roughly 15 per second. In the case of motion pictures, the images are usually presented at 18 frames per second in silent films and 24 frames per second in sound films. In the case of television, the picture is changed either 25 or 30 times a second (25 in the UK and other countries where the mains frequency is 50 Hz and 30 in the USA and other countries where it is 60 Hz).

The principle by which a cine camera operates is shown schematically in Figure 7.1. Although the film is driven through the camera at constant speed by the driving sprockets, it actually passes through the film gate in a series of jerks, with each frame stopping in front of the aperture in the gate just long enough for it to be exposed. Between successive exposures, the film is pulled down through the gate by a claw mechanism which engages the sprocket holes in the film. During these movements, light is prevented from reaching the film by a rotating shutter, which only allows light to pass during the periods when the film is stationary. The two loops of film (above and below the gate) allow the film to move in this intermittent manner without breaking.

When a motion picture film is being projected, exactly the same type of intermittent motion takes place in the projector, light only being allowed to pass through the film during the short periods when each successive frame is held stationary in front of the aperture in the film gate.

The Different Formats in which Cine Materials can be Produced

Although motion pictures are produced in four main film widths or gauges (8 mm, 16 mm, 35 mm and 70 mm) it is only the first two that are used to any great extent in the production of instructional films. Until 1965, virtually all such work was done on 16 mm film, with the narrower 8 mm gauge being almost entirely restricted to amateur 'home movie' making, since it did not produce anything like the quality of pictures that was possible using the wider format. Since 1965, however, a greatly improved type of 8 mm film known as 'super 8' has been available. This has a much larger frame size than the old type of 8 mm film (which is now known as *regular* or *standard* 8 to distinguish it from super 8) and produces a much better picture quality. Thus it represents a perfectly acceptable (and considerably cheaper) alternative to 16 mm film for many instructional purposes. Use of the larger format is advisable where very high quality is required, however, or where the film is to be shown to a large audience (more than 100 or so people). Some of the main features of the two formats are compared in Figure 7.2.

The Different Types of Sound System

Although some cine films are 'silent', others have an associated sound signal. This can either be incorporated in the picture film itself (single-system sound) or carried on a separate medium (double-system sound).

In the case of a single-system sound film, the sound signal is carried on a magnetic or optical sound track that runs down one edge of the film. A magnetic sound track is simply a narrow strip of magnetic oxide similar to that with which audiotapes are coated, and records the sound signal in the same way — ie in the form of variations in magnetic

Feature	Super 8 mm film	16 mm film
Image on film	5.35 mm x 4.01 mm	9.65 mm x 7.21 mm
Number of frames per foot of film	72	40
Usual length of reel of raw film	50 feet	100 feet
Running time of reel at silent speed (18 fps)	3 min. 20 sec.	3 min. 42 sec.
Running time of reel at sound speed (24 fps)	2 min. 30 sec.	2 min. 47 sec.
Type of container in which film is supplied	closed light-proof cartridge; no threading through camera required	open reel; threading through camera required
Facility for built-in sound track	Yes	Yes

Figure 7.2 **Comparison of the super 8 and 16 mm cine formats**

intensity that correspond to the amplitude variations of the sound. The signal is recorded and played back using heads similar to those used in audiotape equipment. An optical sound track, on the other hand, can be of two types, namely a strip of constant optical density whose width is modulated to correspond to the amplitude of the sound signal or a strip of constant width whose optical density is modulated to correspond to the sound. In both cases, the sound is played back by passing light from a small exciter lamp through the sound track on to a photocell, thus producing an electrical signal that corresponds to the sound. Because of the physical impossibility of having the sound recording or playback system in a cine camera or projector in the same place as the aperture in the film gate, the sound in a single-system sound film is recorded several frames in advance of the pictures to which it corresponds (18 in the case of super 8 mm films and 28 in the case of 16 mm films). As we will see later, this can make it difficult to edit such films.

In the case of a double-system sound film, the sound is recorded on a different medium from the pictures — either another sprocketed 'film' carrying a magnetic or optical sound track that runs in parallel with the picture film, or an audiotape. If the latter is used it is necessary to ensure that the sound on the tape is correctly synchronized with the pictures, especially in the case of speech, otherwise the speaker's lip movements may appear to be noticeably 'out of sync' with the sound.

This can be done either by using a synchronizing device in the cine camera or projector to control the movement of the tape or by encoding special synchronizing signals in the tape which ensure that the projector runs at the right speed when the film is being shown.

The Equipment Needed for Cine Photography

As in the case of still photography, the basic item of equipment needed for cine photography is a suitable camera. Typical super 8 mm and 16 mm cine cameras are shown in Figure 7.3.

Figure 7.3 **Super 8 mm (left) and 16 mm cine cameras**

As with still cameras, the cost of cine cameras varies enormously, depending partly on the format and partly on the quality and sophistication of the camera itself. In the case of super 8, a silent camera of reasonable quality can be obtained for as little as £120 and a magnetic sound camera for roughly £400, although it is possible to pay very much more if very high quality and/or sophisticated facilities are required. 16 mm cameras tend to be considerably more expensive than their super 8 equivalents, a reasonably good camera with lip sync facilities costing something of the order of £1200 and a tape recorder suitable for use with it a further £400 or so. Because of the phasing difficulties associated with the editing of 16 mm film that has the original sound recorded directly on the film, most 16 mm sound film is shot using double-system sound, even though the film may well be converted into single-system form after the editing has been completed.

Most cine cameras are supplied fitted with a zoom lens with a 4:1 zoom ratio (the ratio of the longest to the shortest focal length); typical focal length ranges being from 10 mm to 40 mm in the case of a super 8 camera and from 20 mm to 80 mm in the case of a 16 mm camera. Such lenses are perfectly adequate for most shots, although it may be necessary to use special wide-angle or telephoto lenses in certain circumstances. These cost roughly the same as corresponding lenses for still cameras (see page 106).

Other items that you will probably find that you have a need for include the following:

☐ A camera tripod with a smoothly operating pan/tilt head (cost roughly £100).
☐ A photographic light meter (cost roughly £20); even if your camera is of the automatic-setting type, you will probably find such a meter useful for certain shots (eg close-up work, copying or special filming).
☐ A set of two or three photo-flood lights for use in indoor work (cost roughly £200).

Cine Editing

Unless a film has been very carefully planned and shot in sequence, with the editing being carried out 'in the camera' as the shooting proceeds, it is generally necessary to edit the original film. This is done by examining the various lengths of film using an editing bench — an item that can cost anything from £60 to several thousand pounds depending on the facilities that you want it to incorporate. Using such a bench, the various shots that you decide to incorporate in the final film should be carefully identified, cut from the original film, and arranged in separate coded rolls. They should then be spliced together in the required order using a tape or cement splicer. The former is used in much the same way as an audiotape splicing block (see page 129), the ends of the film being aligned on the unit using the guide pins, cut so that they butt end on, and joined using a length of transparent sprocketed splicing tape. A cement splice is made in a similar way, except that the end of the film is overlapped by one frame line, the emulsion scraped off the lower film over the area of overlap, and the ends bonded together using special cement. The two types of splice are shown in Figure 7.4.

ADDING SOUND TO A FILM AFTER EDITING

Once a film has been edited into its final continuity, it is possible to add a magnetic sound track by first sending the film to the laboratory to have a magnetic stripe added to one edge and then recording the sound on this using a magnetic-sound projector. Such projectors can be used to add sound to both super 8 and 16 mm films. If sound is to be added to a film in this way, it is best to use cement splicing and to carry out the splicing work in such a way that the steps on the striped

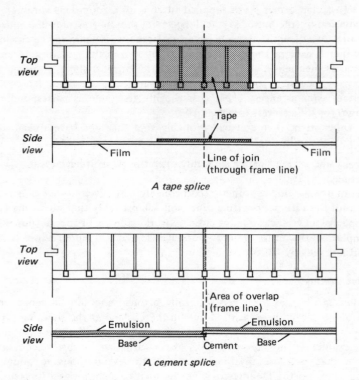

Figure 7.4 **The two ways in which cine film can be spliced**

surface of the film point towards the tail of the film. This enables the magnetic sound head to have a 'smooth ride' over the film, and avoids the clicks that can result if it encounters a cement splice oriented the other way, and has to jump up the step in the film's surface (see Figure 7.5).

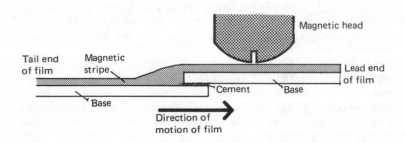

Figure 7.5 **The correct orientation of cement splices in a film with a magnetic stripe**

If a large number of prints of a sound film are required, it is probably advisable to have the sound signal converted into an optical sound track in a laboratory, thus enabling it to be printed on the various copies of the film along with the pictures.

The Basic Principles of Video Recording and Editing

How Television Pictures are Produced

As we saw in the previous section, motion picture films and television both create an illusion of continuous movement by presenting a rapid succession of still images to the eye. In the case of television, these pictures are built up in a series of horizontal lines, British television pictures consisting of 625 such lines and American pictures 525. In order to reduce flicker, a system known as interlaced scanning is employed. In this system, which is shown schematically (in greatly simplified form) in Figure 7.6, a complete scan of the picture is carried out in two stages. Alternate lines (the solid ones in the figure) are

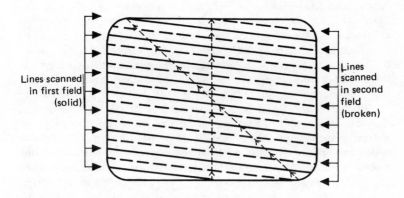

Figure 7.6 **The principle of interlaced scanning**

first scanned in succession, then the scanning process is repeated for the remaining lines (the broken ones in the figure). In the British 625 line system, the scanning of the first field begins at A (the start of line 1) and ends at B (half way along line 313); the scanning of the second field starts at C, beginning by completing line 313 and finishing at D (the end of line 625), after which the scanning process starts again at A. In the American 525 line system, the scanning process is similar, with the transition between the two fields of a frame taking place half way along line 263. In both systems, the field scanning rate is equal to the mains frequency, something that is necessary for technical reasons. Thus, in Britain, the scanning rate is 50 fields (25 frames) a second, while in America it is 60 fields (30 frames) a second.

In a television camera, a system of lenses is used to produce an optical image of the scene being recorded on a mosaic of photo-conductive or photo-emissive cells. This is then scanned by an electronic beam, producing an electrical signal that varies in strength according to the intensity of the light falling on that part of the mosaic. In a colour television camera, three separate scanning processes take place, one for each of the three primary colours used in colour television (red, blue and green).

In a television receiver or monitor, the opposite process takes place, the fluorescent rear surface of the screen being scanned by an electron beam that builds up the picture line by line. In a colour set, three separate scanning systems are again used — one for each of the primary colours — with a special perforated mask being used to ensure that each colour beam strikes the correct parts of the screen.

How Television Signals are Recorded

A television signal consists of three basic components: a high-frequency signal carrying the picture information, a synchronizing signal that controls the scanning process by which this information is converted into a sequence of fields and frames, and an audio signal that carries the sound. The latter two signals can be recorded on magnetic tape in the conventional manner, namely, by using stationary heads to produce tracks running along the length of the tape, but it is not possible to record the picture signal in this way because of the high frequencies that it contains (up to five mega-hertz). The maximum frequency that a tape recording system can handle is proportional to the speed at which the tape moves past the head and inversely proportional to the head gap width. Even using the smallest head gaps that are technically possible, it would be necessary to employ tape speeds of several hundred inches per second in order to record the picture components of television signals in the conventional way, something that is clearly not practicable. Fortunately, this problem can be overcome by employing a rotating head support system that moves the video head(s) rapidly across the tape as it travels through the machine. In most of the videorecorders used for instructional purposes, some form of helical scan system is used. Here, the tape is wound round a cylindrical drum in a manner similar to that shown in Figure 7.7, a drum that rotates at high speed within the loop of moving tape. In the U-wrap system shown in the figure (the configuration used in most video-cassette recorders) the drum carries two heads, diametrically opposite one another. Thus, as the drum revolves, these execute a series of parallel scans across the tape as it moves round the drum. The video signal is therefore recorded in a discontinuous series of stripes, which

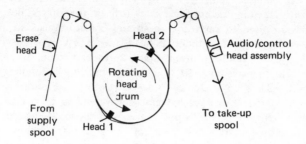

Plan view

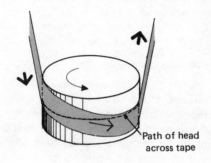

Front view

The configuration of the tape-head system

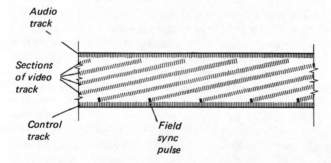

The pattern of tracks on the tape

Figure 7.7 **The principle of helical-scan videotape recording using the U-wrap tape configuration**

can be joined up electronically to produce a continuous signal when the tape is replayed. These diagonal video tracks take up the entire width of the tape except for narrow strips at the top and bottom edges, which are used to carry the audio and control signals in the form of conventional tracks. With a twin-head U-wrap system of the type shown in Figure 7.7, the head drum rotates 25 times a second when recording 625 line pictures and 30 times a second when recording 525 line pictures. Thus, in each case, one complete frame is recorded during each revolution, with each frame corresponding to two segments of video track on the tape — one for each of the two fields that compose it. As shown in the lower part of the figure, the start of the track segment representing each field is labelled with a field synchronizing pulse. These pulses enable the separate segments of the video signal to be properly integrated during the playback process. When the tape is played back, the tape moves through the machine in exactly the same way, the video signal being read off the tape by the rotating video heads, the audio signal by the audio head and the control signal by the control track head. The latter is used to synchronize the movement of the tape with the rotation of the video head so that the intermittent video track is scanned in the correct way.

The Different Videotape Formats

Like motion picture film, videotape is available in a range of widths, in this case 2 inches, 1 inch, ¾ of an inch, ½ an inch and ¼ of an inch. Of these different widths, however, only two are widely used in instructional television work, namely ¾ of an inch and ½ an inch, with the latter being by far the most popular type. The two largest sizes of tape are only used when the work has to be of broadcast standard, while the smallest is only used with a single small non-standardized type of videorecorder.

Half-inch videotape is available both in open-reels (for use with open-reel videotape recorders (VTRs) similar to open-reel audiotape machines) and in sealed cassettes (for use with videocassette recorders (VCRs), which are again similar to their audiotape counterparts). The two most widely used videocassette formats are VHS and Betamax, both of which are primarily designed for domestic use but are perfectly adequate for most educational and training purposes.

Three-quarter inch videotape is used when higher quality is required, and is again available both in open-reel and cassette form. The most widely used videocassette format is U-matic, which is available in two forms: standard or low-band U-matic and high-band U-matic. As its name suggests, the latter has an extended bandwidth compared with the standard form, and thus produces higher quality results; it is, however, considerably more expensive to work with.

The Equipment Needed for Producing Video Materials

At one time, practically all instructional television work was carried out using monochrome (ie black and white) equipment, since (a) colour equipment was prohibitively expensive in comparison, and (b) research had shown that monochrome television was just as effective as colour television for most instructional purposes. Since the mid 1970s, however, colour equipment has become steadily cheaper in real terms, with the result that it has achieved progressively wider use. Indeed, virtually all television equipment now being purchased for educational or training purposes is of this type, with the result that black and white instructional television has, to all intents and purposes, become obsolete. The one exception is time-lapse video recording, which is still largely carried out in monochrome, but this too will no doubt 'go coloured' in due course.

THE BASIC EQUIPMENT NEEDED FOR VIDEO WORK
If you are interested in producing video materials, but do not have

Figure 7.8 **A portable TV camera and linked videocassette recorder system in use**

access to any suitable equipment at the moment, the best way to get started is to acquire a basic colour 'portapack' system. This consists of a portable colour TV camera (with built-in microphone) and a compatible half-inch videocassette recorder, and is usually powered by a portable belt of rechargeable batteries. Of the two standard half-inch VCR formats, VHS is preferable to Betamax because more sophisticated electronic editing facilities are available for use with this type of system. A portable TV camera and VHS recorder similar to those shown in Figure 7.8 can be obtained for around £1200 (£600 for the camera and £600 for the VCR and ancillary equipment). Such a system will enable you to record video materials both outdoors and indoors, although you may well require to use floodlights for some of the latter work (see page 163 for the cost of such lights).

ADDITIONAL EQUIPMENT NEEDED FOR VIDEO EDITING

Unlike audiotape editing, which can be carried out either by cutting and rejoining the tape or by dubbing from one tape on to another, videotape editing can only be carried out by electronic means. The reason for this should be self-evident from Figure 7.7, which shows the complicated overlapping track patterns by which a television signal is recorded on videotape. All videotape editing thus requires the use of at least two videorecorders — one to play back the original material and one to record this on the edited tape.

If you already possess a 'portapack' system of the type described above, purchase of a compatible mains videorecorder (cost roughly £400) will provide you with rudimentary videotape editing facilities. Such a system is not really suitable for producing high-quality edited material, however, since the picture will inevitably break up at the start of each re-recorded sequence, and there may also be slight incompatibilities between the machines, thus causing various forms of noise and distortion to appear. These problems can only be overcome by using a custom-designed videotape editing suite consisting of two compatible high-quality videorecorders linked by a central control unit. A straightforward VHS editing suite like the one shown in Figure 7.9 costs roughly £5000, although it is again possible to pay a great deal more than this if very high-quality or sophisticated facilities are required.

If you have the money available, two useful ancillary items of equipment can be added to your basic editing suite. The first is a time base corrector, an electronic system that stabilizes the video signals being processed by the system, which enables a much higher quality of edited material to be produced. The price of such systems starts at around £3000, although it is possible to pay well over £10,000 for a more sophisticated version. The second is a caption generator (sometimes called an electronic typewriter), a keyboard device that enables captions and other alpha-numeric materials to be added to a television picture by feeding them directly into the video signal. A basic caption generator can be obtained for around £1000, with more sophisticated versions starting at around £3000. If you are producing a large amount of video material, however, such an item can pay for itself in a comparatively short time by cutting down the cost of producing original artwork for captions.

Figure 7.9 **A videotape editing suite**

SETTING UP A TELEVISION STUDIO

Although it is possible to produce excellent instructional video materials using the equipment described above (a single 'portapack' camera/ recorder system plus an editing suite), the range of materials that can be produced is obviously greatly increased if you have access to a properly appointed multi-camera television studio. By using an existing room, a makeshift three-camera colour TV studio can be set up and equipped for roughly £12,000 (£6000 for the ancillary equipment [vision mixer, camera control units, monitors, sound equipment, videorecorder, lights, etc] and £6000 for the cameras and tripods). It is, of course, possible to spend a great deal more than this for a fully equipped custom-built studio with a separate control room. If you are planning a new building or having an existing building re-furbished, this is probably the best time to set up such a facility. The cost may well be obtainable as part of the overall capital sum assigned to the project rather than having to be pleaded for separately (this is how my own unit acquired the television studio facilities shown in Figures 7.10 and 7.11).

Figure 7.10 **The television studio
in RGIT's Educational Technology Unit**

Figure 7.11 **The control room of RGIT's television studio**

Designing and Producing Cine and Video Materials

Deciding Which Medium to Use

The starting point in planning a cine film or video programme should be the realization that there is a definite need for moving visual material of this type in a particular instructional situation — either in a supportive role or as the main vehicle for instruction — and that no suitable material is already available. Once this has been clearly established, a decision should be made as to which of the two media would be more appropriate in the situation in question — cine or video. Here a number of factors will obviously have to be taken into account, including the nature of the instructional process in which the material is to be used, the role that the material is intended to play, the availability (or otherwise) of suitable equipment, facilities and support staff, and — most important of all — your own personal experience, skills and preference.

Having said all this, however, I feel bound to point out that video is now a far easier medium to work with than cine, partly because the editing process is much simpler and partly because it requires no external laboratory support, thus avoiding the annoying delays that such support inevitably entails. Thus, at the risk of offending any cine buffs among my readers, I would strongly recommend the use of video rather than cine for most instructional work. In my own College, for example, video has virtually displaced cine, and the production of video materials for instructional and publicity purposes is now a major 'growth industry' — second only to the development of computer-mediated materials.

Planning the Film or Programme

Once a decision has been reached to produce a cine film or video programme for instructional purposes, the next step should be to draw up a rough plan for the film or programme, outlining its content and basic structure. This should then be converted into a more detailed plan, in which the visual and narrative contents of the different sections are specified. As in the case of a tape-slide programme, such a plan can be produced either in the form of a storyboard (see page 147) or as a script similar to that shown in Figure 6.2. Whichever method is used, however, the following general guidelines should be borne in mind:

☐ Limit the content of the film or programme. Remember that the viewer will only have one chance to understand what is being covered, and cannot ask questions. Thus, if you try to cover too much material or introduce too much detail, some of your audience may become confused or 'get lost'. If this happens, the material obviously has little chance of achieving its design objectives.

☐ Make sure that the film or programme has a definite structure, and that this structure is made clear to the viewers by using appropriate 'signposts and links' — either in visual or in verbal form. Failure to do this can again lead to confusion and consequent failure of the material to achieve its objectives.

☐ Try to keep to a 'linear' argument in each section of the film or programme, avoiding the temptation to go off on diversions or digressions. These can again lead to confusion in a mediated presentation, since the presenter is not in direct touch with his audience and thus has no means of gauging whether they are following his argument and taking appropriate steps if they are not.

☐ Remember that cine and video are both essentially *visual* media, in which the narrative should play a supportive rather than a central role. (If this is not the case, you are probably using the wrong medium to present your material.) Thus, when planning a cine film or video programme, you should *think visual* at all times, building the film or programme round the sequence of pictures that you have decided to incorporate rather than simply using the pictures to support a mediated lecture, as is usually the case with a tape-slide programme (see page 145).

☐ Also remember that cine and video are both *moving* visual media, so that any material produced in these media should generally incorporate *motion* of some sort. (If it does not, then you are again probably using the wrong medium.) Note that such motion can be produced either by movement of the actual subject material or by movement of the camera, change of camera angle, etc during shooting or editing, as we will see later.

☐ Try to keep the visual treatment of the subject matter straight-forward and simple, avoiding 'artistic' or 'gimmicky' shots. These simply distract the viewer from the *content* of the film or pro-gramme, so that the 'medium' gets in the way of the 'message' — a fatal weakness in any mediated instruction system.

☐ Make sure that you get the 'continuity' right, so that the shots follow one another in logical order. For example, if your film or programme shows an actual situation (eg a process or a machine) together with a schematic diagram of the same thing, try to match them up as closely as possible so that the viewer can relate the diagram to the situation that it is supposed to represent. Something that moves from right to left in the former, for example, should move in the same direction in the latter, otherwise viewer con-fusion will almost certainly result.

THE DIFFERENT TYPES OF SHOT THAT CAN BE USED IN A FILM OR VIDEO

Let us now take a brief look at the different visual 'building bricks' that can be used to construct a cine film or video programme, ie the different types of shot.

The three basic types of shot: In all cine and video work, three basic types of shot should form the bulk of most sequences. These are:

1. The *long shot* (LS), which provides a general view of the subject taken from such a distance that the subject is seen in the context of the background or setting in which it is located at the time.
2. The *medium shot* (MS), which provides a closer view of the subject, eliminating most of the background details.
3. The *close-up* (CU), which provides an even closer view of the subject or a specific part thereof, excluding everything else from view.

These three types of shot are illustrated in Figure 7.12. Note that the terms 'long shot', 'medium shot' and 'close-up' do not imply that the shot should be taken from any specific distance, since this will depend entirely on the nature of the subject being shot. A 'long shot', for example, can be taken from several hundred yards in the case of a large building and from a few feet in the case of a piece of equipment of relatively small size. Also different cameramen can interpret the terms in different ways, so that what is a medium shot to one may well be a close-up to another. It is also possible to use shots intermediate to the three basic types [eg a medium close-up (MCU), which is half way between a medium shot and a close-up], or shots which lie beyond the normal LS-MS-CU sequence [eg an extreme long shot (ELS) or extreme close-up (ECU) — see Figures 7.13 and 7.14].

Moving camera shots: As we saw above, it is possible to introduce a sense of movement into a cine or video sequence by moving the camera or changing the effective distance or angle of viewing during shooting. Some of the main options available include the following:

☐ *Zooming* – where the apparent distance from which the scene is shot is increased (zooming out) or decreased (zooming in) during the actual shooting by using a zoom lens (see page 163) and varying its focal length in a continuous manner (not to be confused with dollying).

☐ *Panning* – where the camera is rotated about a vertical axis during the shot, thus causing its effective field of view to sweep across the scene being shot (not to be confused with crabbing).

☐ *Tilting* – where the camera is rotated about a horizontal axis at right angles to the direction of shooting during the shot, thus causing the subject to be scanned in a vertical direction.

☐ *Dollying* (or tracking) — moving the camera towards or away from the subject during the shot.

☐ *Crabbing* (or trucking) — moving the camera along a line at right angles to the direction of shooting during the shot.

Angle and position shots: Another way of introducing special effects or variety into a cine or video sequence is to use different camera angles. Some of the possibilities are again listed below:

Long shot

Long shot

Medium shot

Medium shot

Close-up

Close-up

Figure 7.12 **The three basic types of shot
used in cine and video work**

Figure 7.13
An extreme long shot

Figure 7.14
An extreme close-up

☐ *High-angle shots* — where the camera is above normal eye level, looking down on the subject (this effectively places the subject in an 'inferior' position, reducing its size and slowing down any motion that it may possess).

☐ *Low-angle shots* — where the camera is below normal eye level, looking up at the subject (this places the subject in a dominant position, exaggerating its height and speeding up any movement).

☐ *Subjective shots* — where the camera shoots 'over the shoulder' of the person carrying out the operation being filmed or recorded, thus giving the impression of seeing the operation from that person's point of view (in most shots, the camera views the scene from the point of view of an objective observer).

Producing the Film or Video

When it comes to the actual production of a cine film or video programme, the procedure used will depend on a number of factors, including:

☐ the medium and format being used (super 8 mm cine, 16 mm cine, VHS video, U-matic video, and so on);

☐ the method of recording the associated sound (if any);

☐ whether the material is to be filmed or recorded in a studio or on location;

☐ the detail in which the shooting sequence has been pre-planned;

☐ the method of editing that is going to be employed.

In the case of a cine film, two alternative approaches can be used. The first is to plan the shooting sequence in great detail and then to take the various shots in sequence, so that the editing is effectively carried out 'in the camera'. This is probably the best method to use with super 8 film, where editing can pose problems. The other method is to shoot the various scenes non-sequentially, without making any attempt to edit 'in the camera', and to produce the final edited version of the film afterwards — by cutting and splicing. This is probably the best method to use with 16 mm film where, as we have seen, the original sound is best recorded on a separate system so that it can be added to the actual film once the editing process has been completed.

In the case of a video programme, two similar approaches can be used. The first is to draw up a highly detailed shooting script for the programme and then to carry out the actual shooting in a multi-camera studio, so that the material can be shot sequentially, using a video mixer to 'edit' the programme as the shooting proceeds. This requires meticulous planning and, even then, will probably not 'come off' at the first attempt, so that several re-takes of the entire programme may be necessary. The second method is to use a single portable camera to record the various shots non-sequentially, and then to edit the material into its final continuity using suitable electronic editing facilities. This is probably the most convenient method of producing the majority of instructional video materials, and is the one that we generally employ in my own College. Because of the fact that the picture always breaks up when a videorecorder connected to a camera is stopped and takes some time to stabilize when it is re-started, it is not possible to produce a satisfactory video programme by carrying out intermittent sequential shooting of the type that can be used with a cine camera.

Readers who require more detailed guidance on how to plan and produce cine or video materials are referred to the various specialized publications on the subject listed in the Bibliography. The booklet on the use of portable video equipment published by the Scottish Council for Educational Technology is particularly recommended to newcomers to the video field.

Bibliography

Beal, J D (1974) *Cine Craft.* Focal Press, London & New York.

Coombes, P and Tiffin, J (1978) *Television Production for Education.* Hastings House, New York.

Gibson, T (1972) *Closed-Circuit Television Single-Handed.* Pitman Publishing, London.

Gibson, T (1970) *The Practice of ETV.* Hutchinson Educational Ltd, London.

Kemp, J E (1980) *Planning and Producing Audiovisual Materials.* Harper and Row Publishers Inc, New York (Chapters 23 and 24).

Kinross, F (1968) *Television for the Teacher.* Hamish Hamilton Ltd, London.

Mattingly, G and Smith, W (1973) *Introducing the Single-Camera VTR System: A Layman's Guide to Video Recording.* Scribners, New York.

Mikolas, M and Hoos, G (1976) *Handbook of Super 8 Production.* United Business Publications, New York.

Robinson, R (1974) *The Video Primer.* Quick Fox Inc, New York.

Rowatt, R W (1980) *Video — A Guide to the Use of Portable Video Equipment.* Scottish Council for Educational Technology, Glasgow.

Wilson, A J (1973) *ETV Guidelines. Writing, Directing and Presenting.* Hutchinson Educational, London.

Chapter 8
How to Produce
Computer-Mediated Materials

Introduction

Having completed our examination of all the various 'traditional' types of audiovisual instructional materials, we will now turn our attention to the latest — and, in the opinion of some people, potentially the most important — type: computer-mediated materials. With the advent of the cheap microcomputer, and the prospect of such machines becoming even cheaper and more powerful with every year that passes, there is certainly no doubt that such materials constitute one of the most valuable tools at the disposal of today's teachers and trainers.

Following our usual pattern, we will begin this chapter by discussing the various ways in which computers can be used in different types of instructional situation. Then we will take a fairly detailed look at the design of 'conventional' computer-based learning (CBL) materials, offering guidance on how to produce the various types ('number crunching' and data-processing packages, 'substitute tutor' packages, 'substitute laboratory' packages, and so on). Finally we will take a brief look at what could eventually prove to be the most useful computer-mediated system of all — interactive video.

How Computers can be Used in Different Teaching/Learning Situations

Let us now see how computers can be used in the three broad classes of instructional situation that we have discussed throughout this book — mass instruction, individualized instruction and group learning.

Mass Instruction

To date, the main use of computers in mass instruction has been in a supportive role during conventional expository lessons rather than as a vehicle for mediated exposition, although current developments in the field of interactive video may well cause this situation to change. In such a supportive role, computers can be used in a wide variety of ways, eg:

☐ As vehicles for teaching about computers, and teaching computer programming.

☐ As a means of carrying out complicated calculations or data-processing activities in the course of a lecture, lesson or training session, and of demonstrating these to the class.

☐ As a vehicle for demonstrating simulations of all sorts to a class.

☐ As a means of generating graphical materials and demonstrating these to a class.

☐ As a mode of entry to databases of all types.

Individualized Instruction

Although computers are capable of playing a useful role in mass instruction, their most important potential role in education and training is almost certainly in the area of individualized instruction. Here they probably constitute the most powerful delivery system yet developed and, in the opinion of many commentators, seem likely to bring about changes in education and training that can only be described as revolutionary. The possible future course of this 'computer revolution' is mapped out in detail in an excellent book by Hawkridge (see Bibliography) which should, in my opinion, be set reading for all teachers and trainers — whether they agree with his views or not.

Some of the main ways in which computers can be used in individualized instruction — either on their own or in combination — are outlined below.

USE AS A 'SUBSTITUTE TUTOR'

Here, the learner is guided through an instructional sequence by carrying out an on-line dialogue with a computer via an interactive terminal (usually a keyboard/video display unit). The computer is programmed to present the learner with information, ask questions, and react to the responses by presenting further information or questions. This adaptive style of learning is directly descended from the programmed learning movement of the 1950s and 1960s. It is essentially similar to 'branching' programmed learning, but is capable of being much more sophisticated than the latter because of the greater flexibility and data-handling capacity of computers compared with conventional teaching machines and programmed texts. Tutor-mode computer-assisted learning (CAL) of this type seems certain to play an increasingly important role in education and training during the remainder of this century, and may well bring about the massive swing from conventional expository teaching to mediated individualized learning that some commentators (eg Hawkridge) predict.

USE AS A 'SUBSTITUTE LABORATORY'

In this, the second main CAL mode, the computer is more of a learning resource than a direct instructional device. In this mode, real-life or hypothetical situations of all types can be modelled on the computer, thus allowing the effect on the situation of changing key variables or parameters to be studied by the learner. In this way, learners can be given experience of a far wider range of situations than would be possible by conventional means and can, furthermore, do so in an enactive rather than a passive learning situation — something that always greatly increases the effectiveness of an instructional process. Computer simulations of this type also seem certain to play an increasingly important role in future education and training.

USE IN A MANAGERIAL OR SUPERVISORY ROLE

A third major way in which computers can contribute to individualized learning is by acting as managers or controllers of the learning process. Here the computer does not make a direct contribution to the teaching/learning process, as is the case in computer-assisted learning. Rather it acts in a supportive and/or supervisory role, relieving the teacher or trainer of some of the more tedious or time-consuming tasks normally associated with individualized learning, allowing him to devote more time to meeting the needs of individual learners. Specific ways in which computers can contribute to computer-managed learning (CML) include administration and marking of tests, providing ongoing guidance to learners based on their performance and individual needs, and maintaining up-to-date records of the progress both of individual learners and of the student/trainee body as a whole.

Group Learning

Computers can also make a significant contribution to a wide range of group-learning activities. They can, for example, be used to manage or structure a group-learning process, eg by guiding the group through a simulation exercise of some sort. They can also provide a vehicle through or with which a group of learners can interact, as well as providing facilities for gaining access to databases, performing calculations, investigating simulated situations, generating graphics, etc.

All the above applications of computers in education and training are described in much greater detail in an extremely useful book on educational computing written by Nick Rushby (see Bibliography), and interested readers are referred to this.

How to Produce 'Conventional' CBL Materials

In the remainder of this chapter, we look at the planning and design of computer-based learning materials, dealing first with what might be called 'conventional' CBL materials (to distinguish them from the interactive video materials that are now starting to become available). The design of such materials is, of course, a highly specialized business and, in an introductory book of this nature, I can do no more than offer general guidance on how to set about the task of developing CBL materials of various types. Nevertheless, I hope that this will serve as a useful starting point for readers who are interested in producing such materials.

The Hardware Used in Computer-Based Instruction

A computer can be defined as a device that is able to accept information, apply some processing procedure to it, and supply the resulting new information in a form suitable to the user. Since the first cumbersome valve machines were developed during the late 1940s and early 1950s, the power (ie data-handling capacity) of computers has increased by many orders of magnitude, while the real cost of computers has undergone a steady fall. As a result the use of computers, which was first restricted to a few government agencies and very large firms, has now spread to virtually every sector of human activity. This trend has been greatly accelerated by the development of cheap microcomputers, which continue to become increasingly sophisticated and versatile — and progressively less expensive — every year.

The great majority of modern electronic computers, particularly those that are used for educational and training purposes, are digital computers. These are so called because the information that they handle is converted into digital form (ie expressed in terms of a code based on 0 and 1, the two symbols used in the binary number system) before processing. Such computers are subdivided into three broad classes: mainframe computers, minicomputers and microcomputers.

Mainframe computers are large, highly expensive machines (costing at least several hundred thousand pounds) that normally require a custom-built suite of rooms and a highly trained team of specialist staff to operate them — the sort of machines that are used by large firms and organizations and are installed in the central computer units of universities and major colleges. The larger of the two mainframe machines that are currently installed in my own College is shown in Figure 8.1. This has over 80 terminals, spread over six separate sites, thus enabling all staff to make use of its facilities on a time-sharing basis. Much of the computer-based instruction that is carried out in the College is done using this machine.

Minicomputers are basically simpler, cheaper versions of mainframe machines — the type of computers that might be installed by a small business or college or by a major section of a larger organization. Such machines are also widely used in computer-based instruction.

Finally, microcomputers are small 'desk-top' machines that can be purchased for as little as a few hundred pounds or less, and are the machines that are now finding their way into our schools, colleges, training establishments (and homes) in ever-increasing numbers. My own Unit, for example, recently purchased such a computer — a BBC machine complete with video display unit, tape drive, twin disc drive and printer (see Figure 8.2). The entire system cost less than £1500 and is regularly used for developing computer-based learning materials. The two CBL packages described later in the chapter were in fact developed using this system.

Figure 8.1 **The central processing unit of a typical mainframe computer**

Producing 'Number Crunching' and Data-Processing Packages

The original reason why computers were developed was in order to provide help with complicated calculations and data-processing tasks, and this remains one of their most important roles – in all types of instructional situation. Certainly this is an area where computers can be of considerable assistance to teachers and trainers – particularly those who work in disciplines (such as science, engineering or economics) that involve a lot of calculation or data handling. Computers can, for example, be used to carry out standard calculations and data-processing activities (such as the calculation of the means and standard deviations of sets of raw data and the determination of the slopes of graphs) by using appropriate software packages. They can also be used to process data that is fed directly into them from a piece of equipment or apparatus via a suitable interfacing system – a technique that is finding an increasing number of applications in research and teaching laboratories. In my own College, for example, staff of the School of Physics have recently developed an interface system and software package that enables a Geiger counter to be connected directly to a computer. This enables students to carry out certain experiments on radioactive

Figure 8.2 **A typical microcomputer being used
to design CBL materials**

decay, absorption of ionizing radiation, etc without having to spend
hours tediously accumulating raw data. The computer now does this for
them virtually automatically, thus enabling the students to proceed
rapidly to the interpretation of the data – the part of the work from
which they derive most educational value.

If you are interested in developing a 'number crunching' or data-
processing package of this type, the way in which to set about the task
will obviously depend on a number of factors, including:

☐ The nature of the calculation or data-processing activity to be
  carried out.
☐ The nature of the computer to be used (mainframe, mini or micro?
  make? type of peripherals available? etc).
☐ The extent of your programming ability and experience.

If the calculation or processing activity is a simple one, and you are
confident that you possess the necessary programming skills, the best
way to proceed is probably to 'start from scratch' and write the entire

package yourself. If the job is a difficult or complicated one, on the other hand, or if your programming skills or experience are limited, it will probably pay you to seek advice and/or help — either from a colleague who has more experience of programming than you (eg someone in the computing department of your school or college) or from a professional programmer. Such a person may well be able to direct you to an off-the-shelf software package that will be able to do the job you have in mind either as it stands or after suitable modification or, failing this, will almost certainly be able to help you considerably in the production of the sort of package that you want. The services of professional programmers are now becoming increasingly available to teachers and trainers of all types — either within their own establishments or in outside units (such as teachers' centres) to which they have access — and you should never hesitate to seek their help; it could save you a great deal of time and effort.

When designing a package of the type being considered, it is essential to make it as 'user friendly' as possible — particularly if it is to be used by people who have little knowledge or experience of computers. If at all possible, incorporate any operating instructions in the actual program, so that they are presented automatically when the user switches on the machine and/or calls up the program. In many cases, it is also a good idea to provide the user with a hard copy printout rather than simply a soft copy readout on a VDU screen, but this will obviously depend on the nature of the hardware that is at your disposal.

Once you think that you have got the program working properly, and feel that you have trapped all conceivable errors, it is strongly advisable to ask a colleague to give it a thorough work-out *before* proceeding to the field testing stage. Even experienced programmers sometimes fail to spot errors in their own programs, and are often so close to their work that they are not capable of spotting flaws that are apparent to someone who is not familiar with the system. Asking a colleague to see if a way of crashing your program can be found is often a very effective way of bringing such flaws to light.

A CASE STUDY: THE DESIGN OF A SOFTWARE PACKAGE FOR
THE CALCULATION OF AARR

Let us now take a look at how a specific example of the type of package under discussion was recently developed in my own College — a package for the calculation of the average annual rate of return (AARR) of an offshore oilfield over its producing life. This is typical of the sort of short, simple 'number crunching' package that can be developed by anyone who possesses even rudimentary programming skills in a suitable high-level language such as BASIC or FORTRAN.

Why the package was needed: In 1984 my colleague, Eric Addinall, and I developed a suite of teaching materials on the economics of the offshore petroleum industry for Phillips Petroleum, who wanted to include such materials in a new multi-media educational library that they planned to make available to schools. The suite incorporated over 20 separate class activities — many of them computer-based — and was built around a highly realistic computer simulation of the economics of an offshore field.

In the course of developing these materials, it was necessary for us to devise a simple procedure for calculating the AARR of an offshore field development project. This index (which is also known as the internal rate of return or marginal efficiency of investment of a project) is one of the key economic indicators used by companies like Phillips to assess the likely profitability of fields. It is found by determining the nominal percentage discount (ie inflation) rate which, if in operation throughout the life of the field, would produce zero terminal cumulative real cash flow, ie would make the total discounted income over the life of the field exactly equal to the total discounted expenditure. If the escalated (ie undiscounted) net cash flow for the ith year is ENCF(i), the value of the AARR for a project which lasts for n years is therefore given by the equation:

$$\sum_{i=1}^{n} \frac{\text{ENCF}(i)}{\left(1 + \frac{\text{AARR}}{100}\right)^i} = 0$$

Since this equation has no analytical solution, it is necessary to solve it numerically — hence the need for a computer package to enable the calculation to be carried out in a reasonable time.

The type of package that was produced: What we had to produce was a package that would enable the user to feed in the escalated net cash flow figures for the various years of the project and calculate the AARR value directly from these. Two alternative approaches to the latter were possible. The first would be to program the computer so that it would carry out the entire calculation automatically, going through an iterative process by which it would eventually produce the AARR value. The second would be to make the user play an active part in this iterative process, only using the computer to carry out the 'number crunching' involved at each stage. We eventually decided that the latter approach would have definite educational advantages, and developed a suitable computer program together with a set of instructions on how to use it.

The program that was eventually produced is listed in full in Figure 8.3 together with a sample set of data (lines 1000-1100). This was written in BASIC for a BBC microcomputer and can easily be adapted for use on any of the other makes of microcomputer that are to be found in secondary schools. Note that this program is included purely in order to show readers the sort of applications-type program

```
   10 CLS
   20 PRINTTAB(0,5);:INPUT"INPUT A GUESS FOR 'AARR' AS A PERCENTAGE",I
   30 TR=0
   40 READ N,P
   45 IF N=999 GOTO70
   50 R=P/((1+I/100)^N):TR=TR+R
   60 GOTO40
   70 PRINT TR
   80 IF ABS(TR)<1 GOTO130
   90 IF TR>0 PRINT"YOUR VALUE FOR THE 'AARR' IS TOO LOW":PRINT:PRINT:PRINT:PRIN
T:PRINT"TRY A HIGHER VALUE":INPUT,I:GOTO160
  110 IF TR<0 PRINT"YOUR VALUE FOR THE 'AARR' IS TOO HIGH":PRINT:PRINT:PRINT:PRI
NT"TRY A LOWER VALUE":INPUT,I:GOTO160
  130 PRINT:PRINT:PRINT:PRINT"GOOD!"
  140 PRINT:PRINT" THE AARR FOR THIS FIELD IS ";I;" %"
  150 END
  160 RESTORE:GOTO30
 1000 DATA 1,-36,2,-88.15,3,-94.761,4,-12.963,5,102.567,6,196.498,7,195.88,8,198
.254,9,207.094,10,208.078,11,209.062,12,177.402,13,152.536,14,66.804,15,49.32
 1100 DATA 16,7.957,17,-307.647,18,25.695,999,0
```

Figure 8.3 **The computer program for the calculation of AARR, together with a typical set of data**

that can easily be produced by any teacher or trainer who has acquired even rudimentary programming skills; it is certainly not intended to be taken as an example of a well-structured program of the type that a professional programmer would write, since it contains a number of features (eg several 'GOTO' statements) that would no doubt offend the purists!

How the package is used: To use the package, it is first necessary to key the program into the computer, together with the data on which the program is to operate. In Figure 8.3 this data is listed under lines 1000 and 1100, consisting of pairs of numbers representing the different years in the life of the field (1-25) and the escalated net cash flow figures for these years, expressed in £millions. Note that the data entry terminates with the group '999.0', this being the signal to the computer that the data is complete. Once this has been done, the user keys in the command 'RUN' and the following sequence is initiated.

1. The computer displays the message:
   INPUT A GUESS FOR 'AARR' AS A PERCENTAGE
   ? —
2. The user keys in a value.
3. The computer calculates the terminal discounted net cash flow using the value inputted and applies a test to the same. If the value is positive and greater than a certain value (set at £1 million), the computer prints the figure as a 'remainder' together with the following message:
   YOUR VALUE FOR THE 'AARR' IS TOO LOW
   TRY A HIGHER VALUE
   ? —
   If the value is negative and greater than £1 million, it prints the figure together with the message:
   YOUR VALUE FOR THE 'AARR' IS TOO HIGH
   TRY A LOWER VALUE
   ? —
   If, on the other hand, the modulus of the value is less than £1 million, the computer prints the message:
   GOOD!
   THE AARR FOR THIS FIELD IS — %
4. The user repeats stages 2 to 3 until the correct value is inputted for the AARR, using the messages and remainder values displayed by the computer for guidance. In this way it is usually possible to home in on the correct value in a relatively small number of tries — six or seven at most.

Producing 'Substitute Tutor' Packages

In the type of packages described in the last section, the computer is simply used as a tool to help carry out a specific task — performance of calculations or processing of data. In 'substitute tutor'-mode CBL, on the other hand, the computer takes a much more active role, effectively controlling the process by which the learner is given personal tuition on a particular topic or guided through an instructional or decision-making sequence. A typical example of an interactive dialogue of this type is given in Figure 8.4. Here, the computer is helping a chemistry undergraduate to plan an experiment in physical chemistry. In the dialogue, the student responses are italicized.

You are required to investigate experimentally the chemical equilibrium of the system: $Fe^{3+} + SCN- \rightleftharpoons FeNCS^2$ in order to discover how the equilibrium constant varies as a function of the ionic strength.
You need a method which is both sensitive and discriminating. Which method(s) do you suggest?

I'm sorry, but I haven't a clue

You first need to consider the physical properties of the individual species, or of the system as a whole, which you might use.
What feature do all the species involved have in common?

They are all ionic

Good!
So what method or methods might you choose which makes use of this property?

Conductivity methods

Yes — a conductance method.
Is a conductance method sensitive? (Very, Fairly, Not Very, Not at All)

Very

No. A conductance method is only fairly sensitive.
Is it a discriminating method?

Yes

Conductance methods are only really discriminating when applied to H^+ ions: for all other ions, the readings are rather similar.
Do you want to consider this method further?

No

What other method(s) might be more discriminating and sensitive?

Possibly a colourimetric method

Good. Are colourimetric methods sensitive?

and so on

Figure 8.4 **Extract from a typical tutor-mode CBL dialogue**

THE DESIGN OF CBL MATERIALS – USE OF AUTHORING SYSTEMS

There are two basic ways in which it is possible to approach the task of designing a tutor-mode CBL package. The first – and most obvious – method is to design the instructional process first and then produce a computer program that can be used to administer this instructional process. If you possess the necessary programming skills (or have access to the services of someone who does) then there is no reason why you should not be able to produce perfectly acceptable CBL materials in this way, although it will probably take you a relatively long time to do so. The second method is to make use of a suitable authoring language or authoring system to help you produce the material. These are specially designed so as to enable people with little or no knowledge of computer programming to produce CBL materials by providing a variety of standard structures within which the materials can be developed. These undoubtedly constitute the easiest and most cost-effective method of developing tutor-mode CBL materials. A wide range of such authoring languages and systems is now available, for use on virtually all types of computers. Detailed information on those that were available in 1983 are given in Dean and Whitlock's *Handbook of Computer-Based Training* (see Bibliography), but this is almost certainly now out of date, since new systems are being developed all the time. Thus my advice to any reader who is interested in using an authoring language or authoring system to develop CBL materials is to seek the advice of a professional programmer or computer consultant; such a person will be able to direct you to the system that is best suited for your particular needs.

Examples of the sort of facilities that authoring systems provide: In order to show readers the sort of materials that can be produced using a suitable authoring system, details of two of the standard models that are available in one such system – the 'PLATO Stand-Alone Author and Delivery System' developed by Control Data – are given below.

The first, the 'Drill and Practice Model', is shown in Figure 8.5. This has the following three stages:

(i)   The learner is shown a title page and introduction (created by the author) and is then given a standard set of instructions on how to use the lesson.

(ii) The learner is set a series of questions created by the author; these can either be presented in a predetermined sequence or culled at random from a bank of questions.

(iii) The computer determines the percentage of correct answers and, using criteria set by the author, directs the learner either to move on to the next stage of the instructional process or to repeat the lesson.

A second PLATO model, the 'Tutorial Lesson Model', is shown in Figure 8.6. This has the following five stages:

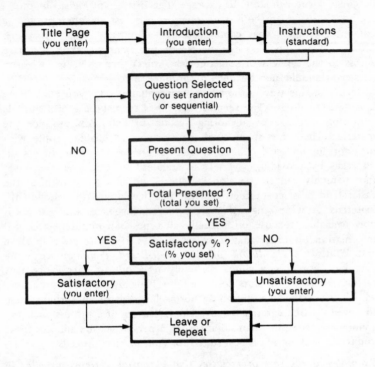

Figure 8.5 **The 'Drill and Practice Model' available
in the PLATO authoring system**

(i)   The learner is presented with a brief introduction to the area to
      be studied, written by the author.

(ii) A menu is displayed, allowing the learner to choose from a
      number of specific topics in the area in question (selected by the
      author).

(iii) Having chosen a topic, the learner is presented with instructional
      information (written by the author) relevant to that topic.

(iv) The learner is asked a diagnostic question (written by the author)
      designed to determine whether or not the instructional
      information has been mastered.

(v)   If the answer is satisfactory, the learner is told to proceed to the
      next topic that he wants to study (again chosen from the menu
      displayed in Stage (ii)); if not, the learner is advised to review
      the lesson material before trying again.

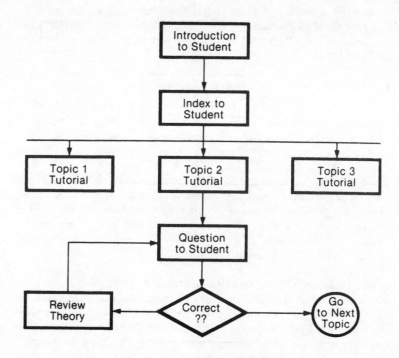

Figure 8.6 **The 'Tutorial Lesson Model' available
in the PLATO authoring system**

Note that most authoring systems provide facilities for sequences
written in conventional programming languages such as BASIC and
FORTRAN to be included in the instructional sequence, and that many
also allow graphic materials to be incorporated. The exact nature of the
facilities available varies considerably from system to system, with the
sophistication of the facilities tending to increase with that of the
hardware with which it is designed to be used. Thus systems designed
for use with inexpensive general-purpose microcomputers tend to be
far less sophisticated than those designed for use on mainframe machines
or machines that have been specially developed for CBL work (eg the
specialized microcomputers used in the PLATO system). Nevertheless
such simple systems are often all that is required to produce perfectly
adequate CBL materials. Owners of BBC microcomputers, for example,
will probably find that the MICROTEXT authoring system that is

available from the National Physical Laboratory is capable of meeting most of their needs.

Readers who are interested in producing tutor-mode CBL materials will find detailed guidance on how to design the materials in the books by Dean and Whitlock and by Godfrey and Sterling that are listed in the Bibliography.

Producing 'Substitute Laboratory' Packages

As we have seen, 'substitute laboratory' CAL packages, in which learners are given experience of situations or enabled to investigate systems via the medium of computer simulations, seem likely to play an increasingly important role in education and training. In the various branches of science and engineering, for example, they can be used to provide instructional and training experiences that would simply not be practicable using conventional methods on grounds of cost, time, safety, etc (eg experiments in genetics or work with systems such as nuclear reactors). Computer simulations can also prove useful in the various social sciences, as well as in business management and commercial, industrial and military training.

HOW TO DESIGN 'SUBSTITUTE LABORATORY' PACKAGES

As in the case of 'substitute tutor' CBL materials, there are two basic approaches that can be adopted to the design of a 'substitute laboratory' package. The first is to begin by deciding on the main features of the situation or system of which you want the learners to be given experience, and then to develop a computer model that incorporates these various features using a conventional high-level programming language such as BASIC or FORTRAN. The second is to make use of a suitable authoring system or special simulation language that incorporates a standard framework in which a model of the type you want can be developed, and to work within this context. If you possess the necessary programming skills, and the system to be simulated is a relatively simple one, the first approach may well be the better way to proceed. With more complicated systems, on the other hand, use of a specialized simulation language or authoring system could offer distinct advantages. Again, my advice to readers who are interested in making use of facilities of this type is to seek the advice of a professional programmer or computer consultant.

Example of the sort of facilities that simulation authoring systems provide: In order to illustrate the sort of facilities that can be provided via CBL authoring systems, let us again look at one of the standard models that are available in one such system — the 'Situation Simulation Model' from the PLATO system. This model, which is shown in Figure 8.7, enables highly complicated branching decision-making simulations to be developed, and again requires no programming experience on the part of the author. As can be seen from the figure, the learner is first confronted with a situation of the type that he might encounter in real life (devised by the author) and asked to state what action he would take (from a number of alternatives chosen by the author). The learner is then confronted with the new situation that would arise as a result of this action, and again asked to state what he would do. The process is repeated as often as necessary. Other authoring systems such as MICROTEXT offer similar facilities for the modelling of situation simulations of this type.

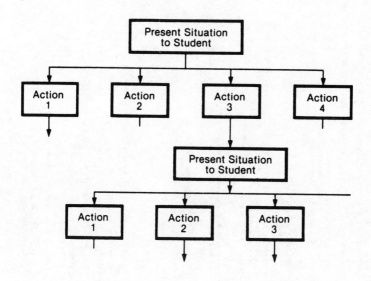

Figure 8.7 **The 'Situation Simulation Model' available in the PLATO authoring system**

Producing supportive courseware for computer simulations: One important difference between tutor-mode and laboratory-mode CBL packages is that the former are generally completely free-standing, with the computer presenting all the relevant information to the learner, whereas the latter usually include supportive courseware — often in the form of a 'user's manual'. The need for such courseware stems from the different role that the computer plays in laboratory-mode CBL, where (as we have seen) it is more of a learning resource than a vehicle for mediated instruction. Thus there is often a need to give the user instructions or guidance on how to use the resource, eg by suggesting possible

```
5 MODE7
10 V=50:A=45:F=0:G=9.81
20 PRINTTAB(9,10);CHR#141;CHR#131;"PROJECTILE MOTION"
30 PRINTTAB(9,11);CHR#141;CHR#131;"PROJECTILE MOTION":FORT=0TO10000:NEXT
40 CLS
50 PRINTTAB(0,8);"The motion of a projectile depends upon":PRINT:PRINT" a) t
he initial velocity,"
60 PRINT:PRINT"    b)  the angle of elevation,"
70 PRINT:PRINT"    c)  the effect of air resistance,"
80 PRINT:PRINT"    d)  the acceleration due to gravity"
90 PROCpage
110 MODE1
120 VDU24,0,500;1279;1023;:VDU28,0,31,39,18
130 COLOUR129:CLS
140 VDU19,0,4,0,0,0:GCOL0,2:CLG
150 CLS:@%=131594:PRINT:PRINT"A..initial velocity.............= ";V
160 PRINT"B..angle of elevation............= ";A
170 PRINT"C..coeff. of air resistance...= ";F
180 PRINT"D..acceleration due to gravity.= ";G:@%=10
190 PRINT:PRINT"To change a parameter:-"
200 PRINT"press A,B,C or D"
210 PRINT:PRINT"To confirm these values, press RETURN"
220 PRINT:PRINT"To end the program press...E"
230 *FX15,0
240 S$=GET$
250 IFS$<>"A"ANDS$<>"B"ANDS$<>"C"ANDS$<>"D"ANDS$<>CHR#13ANDS$<>"E"THEN240
260 IFS$="A"THEN400
270 IFS$="B"THEN500
280 IFS$="C"THEN600
290 IFS$="D"THEN700
300 IFS$=CHR#13 THEN800
305 IFS$="E"THEN910
400 CLS
405 PRINT:PRINT:PRINT"Enter new initial velocity (1-100)"
410 INPUT V
415 IFV<1ORV>100:PRINT"OUT OF RANGE!!":GOTO405
420 FORT=0TO100:NEXT:CLS:GOTO150
500 CLS
505 PRINT:PRINT:PRINT"Enter new angle of elevation (10-80)"
510 INPUT A
515 IFA<10ORA>80:PRINT"OUT OF RANGE!!":GOTO505
520 FORT=0TO100:NEXT:CLS:GOTO150
600 CLS
605 PRINT:PRINT:PRINT"Enter new coeff. of air resist. (0-0.2)"
610 INPUT F
615 IF F<0ORF>0.2:PRINT"OUT OF RANGE!!":GOTO605
620 FORT=0TO100:NEXT:CLS:GOTO150
700 CLS
705 PRINT:PRINT:PRINT"Enter new accel. due to gravity (1-20)"
710 INPUT G
715 IFG<10RG>20:PRINT"OUT OF RANGE!!":GOTO705
720 FORT=0TO100:NEXT:CLS:GOTO150
```

```
800 CLS:PRINT:PRINT:PRINT:PRINT"Press key Z to see the trajectory"
810 *FX15,0
820 X$=GET$
830 IFX$<>"Z"THEN820
840 CLS:PROCtrajectory
860 PRINT:PRINT:PRINT"Press key Z to continue":PRINT"Press key G to clear grap
h area":PRINT"Press key E to end."
870 *FX15,0
880 Z$=GET$
890 IFZ$<>"Z"ANDZ$<>"G"ANDZ$<>"E"THEN880
900 IFZ$="Z"GOTO150
905 IFZ$="G"THEN CLG:CLS::GOTO860
910 END
1000 DEFPROCtrajectory
1010 C=COS(RAD(A)):S=SIN(RAD(A)):SS=SIN(A*2)
1020 MOVE79,500:DRAW79,1000:MOVE1279,500:DRAW79,500
1035 T=0.01:X=0:YY=0
1045 IF F<>0THEN1500
1055 REPEAT
1065 X=v*T*C
1075 Y=v*T*S-0.5*(G*T*T)
1085 PLOT5,X+79,Y+500
1095 IFY>0 THEN T=T+0.02
1105 IF Y-YY>0THENYY=Y
1115 IF Y>0 XX=X
1125 UNTIL Y<0:GOTO1600
1500 REPEAT
1530 X=(V*C/F)*(1-EXP(-F*T))
1540 Y=1/F*(G/F+V*S)*(1-EXP(-F*T))-(G*T/F)
1550 PLOT5,X+79,Y+500
1560 IFY>0 THEN T=T+0.02
1570 IF Y-YY>0THEN YY=Y
1580 IFY>0 XX=X
1590 UNTIL Y<0
1600 CLS:@X=131594:PRINT"A..initial velocity............= ";V
1610 PRINT"B..angle of elevation........= ";A
1620 PRINT"C..coeff. of air resistance..= ";F
1630 PRINT"D..acceleration due to gravity.= ";G
1640 PRINT:PRINT"Range.................= ";XX;" metres"
1650 PRINT"Maximum height..........= ";YY;" metres"
1660 PRINT"Time of flight..........= ";T;" seconds":@X=10:ENDPROC
6000 DEFPROCpage
6010 PRINTTAB(0,30);CHR#136;CHR#130;"Press any key to continue";CHR#137:IF GET$
="":CLS
6020 ENDPROC
```

Figure 8.8 The computer program for the projectile motion simulation

'experiments' that might be carried out using the model round which the package is built. In some cases (eg situation simulations of the type illustrated in Figure 8.7) no such supportive courseware may be necessary, but in others (eg simulations of physical, biological, social or economic systems with several independent variables) the user's guide may be just as important a component of the package as the computer model itself. Thus great care should always be taken in the planning and design of such a document, since the ultimate success of the package as a teaching tool may well depend on it.

A CASE STUDY: THE DESIGN OF A CBL PACKAGE SIMULATING PROJECTILE MOTION

The origin of the package: When planning this chapter, I discussed with Eric Addinall (who is a member of the staff of RGIT's School of Physics) the possibility of developing a simple physics-based simulation for use as a case study. This, I felt, would help to give readers an idea of what the production of such a package involves. We decided that projectile motion would make an ideal subject for such a simulation, with the added advantage that the resulting package would prove useful to our own physics students. We also decided that the simulation would be designed for use on a BBC microcomputer — the standard machine used in the School of Physics for undergraduate work — and would be written in BASIC, since there appeared to be no great advantage in using a specialized simulation language or authoring system in this particular case. We agreed that he would develop the computer model for the package, after which we would collaborate on the preparation of a suitable user's manual. The times taken to complete each stage of the work would be carefully noted.

Preliminary work — deciding on the overall structure and format of the simulation: Before work could start on the computer model, it was necessary to decide what the overall structure of the simulation should be and in what format the material should be presented. With regard to the former, we decided that the package would simulate the motion of a projectile fired over horizontal ground, with the independent variables being the velocity of projection (v), the angle of elevation (θ), the acceleration due to gravity (g) and the air resistance (F). With regard to the format of presentation, we decided that the top half of the VDU field would show the trajectory of the projectile, with the bottom half being used to present instructions and information. This stage of the work took roughly half an hour.

Development of the computer model: Once the above decisions had been made, Eric Addinall was able to start work on the computer model that was to form the heart of the package. The work took just under eight hours, and resulted in the development of the program that is presented in full in Figure 8.8. (Note that this should again be regarded as a typical applications program written by an 'enthusiastic amateur' rather than an example of elegant programming, which it manifestly is not.) The program tells the user what the independent variables are, plots the trajectory that results if these variables are given certain values (eg initial velocity $500\,\text{ms}^{-1}$; angle of elevation $45°$; coefficient of air resistance 0; acceleration due to gravity $9.81\,\text{ms}^{-2}$), and gives the range (R), the maximum height achieved (H) and the time of flight (T). It then invites the user to make any changes to the variables required, plotting the new trajectory and giving the new range, etc for each set of values chosen. All the trajectories so plotted are retained on the screen until the user orders the field to be cleared, thus allowing visual comparisons of different trajectories to be made.

Development of the user's manual: Once we were satisfied with the computer model, we wrote the user's manual for the package. This contained the following sections:

☐ A general description of the simulation and how to become familiar with its use.

☐ Background information on the theory of projectile motion (a) ignoring air resistance and (b) taking air resistance into account.

☐ Instructions on how to use the model to carry out a series of simulated experiments, such as the one described below.
   'Keeping v and g constant (at $50\,\text{ms}^{-1}$ and $9.81\,\text{ms}^{-2}$ respectively), plot R against θ (i) for zero F
                            (ii) for finite values of F from 0.01 to 0.2 in
                                 suitable steps.
   Use the resulting family of curves to plot θ_m (the elevation that produces maximum range) against R.
   Try to explain the results in terms of the theory of projectile motion.'

Writing the user's manual took roughly the same time as developing the computer model, so that the total time needed to produce the complete package was roughly 16 hours — a figure that I hope will give would-be CBL designers some encouragement. The package is now in regular use in RGIT's School of Physics, where it forms the basis of a three-hour laboratory session.

Producing Computer-Managed Learning Packages

In computer-managed learning (CML), we have seen that the computer is used in a managerial or clerical role rather than taking a direct part in the actual process of instruction. Specifically, it can be used:

☐ To generate, administer, mark and analyse tests for diagnostic and/or assessment purposes.

☐ To provide individual guidance to learners about such things as choice of modules, choice of route through a course, and whether or not remedial work is required.

☐ To maintain an up-to-date record of the progress and performance of all the individual students or trainees on a course, so that a tutor or instructor can see how any particular learner is doing at any time.

☐ To provide an ongoing overview of the progress of the student body as a whole, or on the operation of the course in general, to the people responsible for running and planning a course.

Because of the complexity of even a modest CML system, anyone contemplating making use of such a system would be well advised to try to find an existing software package that is capable of doing the job rather than trying to develop his own package 'from scratch'. Needless to say, the advice of a professional programmer or computer consultant should again be sought, since such a person may be able to recommend a suitable package — or a package that can be adapted to do the job required.

Readers who want to find out more about computer-managed learning are referred to the book by Rushby listed in the Bibliography; Chapter 4 of this deals with the subject in some detail.

How to Produce Interactive Video Materials

It is now generally accepted that interactive video constitutes the most powerful medium for mediated instruction yet developed, combining, as it does, the facilities of computer-based learning with those of television. Using such a system, which interfaces an interactive computer terminal with a random-access videotape or videodisc recorder and a television monitor, the author of a CBL programme is no longer restricted to the use of conventional computer graphics which, for all the advances made during recent years, are still severely limited in the extent to which they can represent real-life situations satisfactorily. Rather, he can build high-quality television pictures into his programme (complete with sound track, if required) so that an appropriate sequence can be called up from the videorecorder by the computer whenever it is needed. Needless to say, such a facility adds a completely new dimension to computer-based learning.

The Components of an Interactive Video System

The essential features of an interactive video system are shown schematically in Figure 8.9. As can be seen, the heart of the system is a suitable microcomputer that is connected to a random-access videorecorder by special interfacing equipment. The videorecorder can be either a videotape machine (usually a special videocassette recorder with twin audio tracks) or a videodisc machine (usually an optical videodisc player). Most early interactive video work was done using videotape, but videodisc-based systems (which are capable of handling much more sophisticated programmes) are now becoming increasingly widely used.

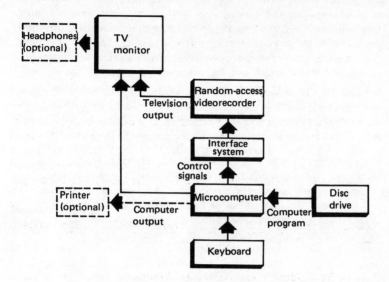

Figure 8.9 **The different components
of an interactive video system**

In both types of system, the content of the programme (the course-ware) is stored on two separate media — the video component being stored on a videocassette or videodisc and the computer component (ie the frames of the CBL sequence into which the video material is built) being held on a floppy disk. The latter also carries the 'system software' (the computer programs that control the presentation of the two types of material to the user). The outputs of both the computer and the videorecorder are fed into a television monitor, usually fitted with headphones if the system is being used for individual study. Some systems also include a printer, which can be used to provide the user with a hard-copy printout of any of the computer-generated material of which a permanent record is required. In all interactive video systems, the user communicates with the computer via a keyboard or keypad.

The Different Methods of Producing Interactive Video Programmes

At the time of writing, most educators and trainers who want to develop their own interactive video materials 'in-house' are more-or-less restricted to the use of a videotape-based system of some sort. Only those who work in a very large organization or have access to massive external funding can hope to produce videodisc-based materials, since the equipment required is not only expensive but also requires highly specialized technical support for its proper use. Detailed inform-ation about what the development of such materials involves can be found in the CET Working Paper by Duke that is listed in the Biblio-graphy, and interested readers are referred to this.

As in the case of conventional CBL materials, the development of videotape-based interactive video materials can be tackled in two ways. If you possess the necessary electronic and programming skills, there is nothing to stop you from connecting a standard microcomputer (such as an Apple II) to a suitable videocassette recorder (eg a U-matic or industrial VHS machine) via special interfacing circuits, and converting conventional video sequences into interactive video programmes using the resulting system. This is probably the cheapest way of producing interactive video materials but is certainly not the easiest, since fairly intimate knowledge of the system and advanced programming skills are required. Thus anyone who does not possess such knowledge and skills would be well advised to make use of a custom-built interactive video authoring facility. A number of systems of this type, which enable people with no knowledge of electronics or programming to develop highly sophisticated interactive video materials, are now available commercially. One such system — the Computer Audio Video Instruction System (CAVIS) developed by CAVIS-Scicon, is shown in Figure 8.10. This is a dual-purpose facility that can serve both as an authoring system for the creation of interactive video materials and as a work station for the study of such materials by individual students or trainees. The photograph shows the system being used in the former mode; when used in the study mode, the large keyboard shown in use in the photograph is replaced by a simple keypad (seen at the right-hand side of the photograph, on top of the control cabinet that contains the videocassette recorder, computer, and interfacing equipment). At the time when this book was written (mid-1984), a complete CAVIS system cost just under £13,000.

How to Develop Programmes

Let us now conclude this discussion of interactive video by taking a broad look at what the design and production of an interactive video programme involves.

THE DESIGN PHASE
This is similar in many ways to the design of a conventional CBL programme, involving the following stages:

☐ Establishment of the exact instructional role that the programme is to fulfil, including detailed formulation of its design objectives.
☐ Deciding on the overall structure and content of the programme and establishment of an outline plan for the same.
☐ Development of the detailed structure of the programme, showing how the CBL and video elements will interrelate; detailed design of the CBL and video materials.

Figure 8.10 **A typical interactive video authoring facility —
the CAVIS system**

THE PRODUCTION PHASE
This also involves three stages, namely:

☐ The production of the video components of the programme and
editing of the same into the final continuity required; this should be
done by the methods described in Chapter 7.

☐ The creation of the various frames of the CBL sequence into which
the video materials are to be integrated using suitable computer
equipment (eg a custom-designed interactive video authoring facility
such as the CAVIS system).

☐ The integration of the video and CBL components to form the final
programme. As explained above, by far the easiest way to do this is
again to use a specialized authoring facility such as CAVIS, which
enables video materials to be converted into interactive form by
people with no programming skills. Indeed, use of such a system
makes the production of the final programme one of the easiest
parts of the entire development process.

Readers requiring more detailed guidance on how to develop interactive
video materials are referred to the books by Duke and Parslow that are
listed in the Bibliography, and also to the Research Report by Bryce.

Bibliography

Bryce, C (1982) *Improved CAI by the use of interfaced random-access
audio-visual equipment.* Dundee College of Technology Research
Report P/24/1.

Dean, C and Whitlock, Q (1983) *A Handbook of Computer-based Training*. Kogan Page, London/Nichols Publishing Co, New York.

Duke, J (1983) *Interactive Video: Implications for Education and Training*. Working Paper no 22, Council for Educational Technology, London.

Godfrey, D and Sterling, S (1982) *The Elements of CAL*. Reston Publishing Co, Virginia.

Hawkridge, D (1982) *New Information Technology in Education*. Croom Helm, London.

Laurillard, D M (1982) The potential of interactive video. *Journal of Educational Television*, **8**, 3, 73.

O'Shea, T and Self, J (1983) *Teaching and Learning with Computers*. Harvester Press, Brighton.

Parslow, E (1984) *Interactive Video*. John Wiley, Chichester.

Rushby, N\J\ (1979) *An Introduction to Educational Computing*. Croom Helm, London.

Further information about the PLATO authoring system mentioned in the text can be obtained from Control Data, Control Data House, 179-199 Shaftesbury Avenue, London WC2H 8AR.

Further information about the MICROTEXT system can be obtained from the Division of Information Technology and Computing, National Physical Laboratory, Teddington, Middlesex TW11 0LW.

Further information about the CAVIS interactive video system can be obtained from Scicon Ltd, Wavendon Tower, Wavendon, Milton Keynes MK17 8LX.

Keyword Index